Forg̲ ̲ ̲ ̲ ̲ ̲

Heroes

The story and war record of Alfred, just one of such forgotten heroes of which there are many to be found in all the armed forces who fought in the second world war.

George Gebauer

www.newgeneration-publishing.com

 New Generation Publishing

I dedicate this book

to all ranks in all the branches

of the armed forces from all

Countries involved in the second

World War.

Acknowledgements

I need to acknowledge those who made this book possible.

It began when my nephew Guenter in Australia, Alfred's youngest son, send me a brief record of his father's war record. Having looked at it and read it through I thought one can write a book about it and I did.

In no particular order, I begin with the proof readers in alphabetical order; Jeanette Collett who also did the final edit. Glenda Edmondson, Barry Jarman and Peter Upward.

The cover of the book was designed and painted by Lesley Stevens.

I give grateful thanks to June Ward and her brother Paul Horton for giving me access to their father's war diary which was of enormous help to me when writing the account of the "Battle of Crete."

Eternal thanks to my dear friend Mike Tanner who again made sure I set the right course to make it easy for the reader to follow the story, as he did with my first book; "From Hitler Youth to Church of England Priest." Published by Amazon 6 years ago and still selling.

A great deal of information and knowledge I acquired from reading articles in newspapers, magazines and watching documentaries about the WW2 on television.

Finally my thanks to Roger Clear for his help getting this book to the publishers and printed.

Contents

Prologue

Now that I am retired and find myself with time on my hands, I have been looking back on my life and all the things I have experienced. What comes to the fore quite frequently is the Second World War and the immediate post war years.

Having lived through and taken part in it, I sometimes look back and wonder what happened to the lads, who shared my experience in the German Armed Forces, and where are they now?

In particular, what happened to the lads I met and shared life with in the P. O. W. Camps on both sides of the Atlantic, ranging from the Balkans Campaign, to Rommel's Africa Corps, to D-Day and thereafter?

When in Ganger Camp, Romsey, Hampshire England, I met a fellow P.O.W. Alfred Zollman by name who became a very good friend of mine. It is his story I would like to tell. Alfred never talked much about his life or his war experiences nor his family background. In fact it was several years after his death, when corresponding with his youngest son in Australia, that this story came to light and I felt the urge to write it down in book form for the world to know about the bravery of the men and women in all the armed forces of all the nations involved in this unhappy war. These heroes came from around the globe. This is another reason why I wrote this book; to make known to the reader of the hardship and endurance suffered by the soldiers in fighting to defeat a tyrant obsessed with the idea to rule the world.

What you read is based on fact although I allowed myself some licence to make the book readable in all parts of the world. The accounts described are real. Thousands of military personnel will have had similar experiences.

[Please note, in order to hide their real identities fictional names are used throughout this book as some are still alive today.]

Chapter 1: Life before and leading up to the Second World War

In April 1941, Alfred Zollman was in the Parachute Pioneer Battalion at Gardelegen assembled for inspection on the parade ground fully equipped and ready for action, to be deployed to the Balkans. Alfred had volunteered soon after his 18th birthday to join the German air force and was called up in April 1940. After 8 weeks training in Frankfurt he felt that this branch of the German Wehrmacht was not for him and requested to be transferred to the Parachute Regiment. It was on the day of his 19th birthday that he was told his request had been granted and he was transferred to the parachute training ground at Standal. Alfred could not have wished for a better birthday present. After 8 weeks of basic training he was transferred for more intense training at Gardelegen.

Here he was with all the other lads he trained so hard with for this moment ready to go forth to fight to prevent further advances up the Balkans, by British forces moving towards central Europe. The Battalion had had some leave earlier before beginning the final training for the battles that lay ahead. German forces had been successful on all fronts so far and occupied much of central and southern Europe. Apart from

Switzerland in central Europe, there were few other countries not occupied for reasons best known to the German government. Sweden and Finland in the far north-east of the Baltic and in the north west Iceland and most of the UK of course. In the far west of Continental Europe, Portugal and Spain. All the boys were keen and looking forward to playing their part in the victorious outcome of the war. They knew each other well as they had been living and training together for nearly a year. Morale was high and why not? After all they were told they were the best. They were selected because of their physical fitness and intelligence to lead the attacks on vital objectives such as Crete later in the year, after the campaign on the Greek mainland had been successfully completed. What's more, their equipment was the most lavish and the best available at the time. If there was any weakness, it was the soldiers very youth and the fact that comparatively few had as yet faced the challenge of battle. Their destinations were Corinth and Athens, including Piraeus. On this front they were most likely to receive the baptism of fire. The rest of the regiment stayed behind to follow them later. Inspection over, the command: "Right turn! Forward march!" and they were on their way to the railway station, singing patriotic songs as they were marching. At the station two trains were waiting to take them and some of their equipment on the two-day journey south to help the forces already there to face the British units that had been drafted in to help the hard pushed Greek forces. Once the excitement had worn off, Alfred settled down and began to think of home. After all, there was a 50/50 chance, he would not come out alive from this battle. With that thought in mind Alfred shut his eyes and looked back over his young life.

On the journey through the Balkans and down the Peninsular towards Greece Alfred could not help but think of his childhood and schooldays. His school days in the little town in which he was born and grew up were happy and carefree. He was born on 2nd June 1921 in the Province of Silesia in the district of Kreis Munsterberg in eastern Germany in a little place called Giesdorf. Alfred did well at school partly because he had a sharp mind and could remember things almost down to the last detail. Sitting exams did not bother him at all as usually he finished up among the top three.

When Hitler came to power Alfred was 11 years old and living in a country town where people were not quite so much affected by the change of regime in the early stages as in the bigger towns and cities. Even so, Alfred was impressed by what he heard on the radio and what he read in the newspapers of what Hitler had to say to the German people. He told them he would break the chains put on Germany by the Treaty of Versailles: "We will not be dictated to by the Gnomes of Zurich. Fight for freedom and prosperity." Alfred knew what poverty was as he had lived through it during the depression experienced of the twenties and thirties. He was impressed by Hitler's words. Here was someone who was courageous enough to tackle these things. On leaving school, life changed unbelievably. Gone were the carefree days roaming through the countryside, swimming in the lake or boating on the river Oder. As a trade, Alfred chose to become a chimney sweep, a sought-after trade in Germany at that time. Many buildings in towns and cities were 4 or 5 storeys high and their chimneys and flues needed to be swept at least once a year. What a man needed for this job was a head for heights as well as a good knowledge of the architecture of the buildings in order to sweep flues thoroughly. His head for heights may well have been one of the reasons Alfred volunteered to join the Luftwaffe.

However, his career as chimney sweep was short-lived as one day when Alfred was a little over-ambitious, he slipped off the roof and broke a leg. That dented his confidence and after a while he resigned and took on several jobs on farms, factories and, finally, in an engineering firm as a carriage builder. In the last letter he had from home his mother wrote that his father was alright and that his two brothers were doing well in their apprenticeships. Rudy would qualify as a motor mechanic in the autumn and Karl, who still had 18 months of training to do was doing well as an electrician. Heidi, Alfred's girlfriend had looked in the other day and asked after him. Ah yes, Heidi, Alfred sighed, the girl of his dreams. She caused him many a sleepless night. She was his pin-up now and he had a picture of her in his pocket close to his heart. Not a day went by when he did not take it out of his jacket and look at the picture fondly and lovingly kissed her pretty face. Yes she was beautiful and Alfred considered himself lucky and very privileged that she had taken a shine to him, for he knew he was not the only one in the pack of young men that made eyes at her. Alfred and Heidi had known each other from school days and lived not all that far apart. Alfred wondered whether they would ever see each other again. Before he was called up they saw each other most weekends as there was no time or opportunity during the week. Friday and Saturday nights they spent with mutual friends, mostly in each others houses. As dancing in public was not allowed in those days there was only one alternative, roll back the carpet and dance at home often late into the night. His love was true love. He saw and knew he had something precious. At the moment he and most of his comrades, as far as he could tell, were still inexperienced in intimate love. 'Virgin Soldiers' in fact. There were one or two who bragged that they had one night stands with a number of girls, but Alfred had his doubts.

Chapter 2: The first experience of war

After two days travelling by train they arrived at their destination and after a short rest and a substantial meal were told that three miles ahead of them was the Greek and British defence line and that they would be in action later in the afternoon to push the enemy as far back as they could before nightfall. There was no need to be told that they were close to the front line as they could see for themselves by what was going on around them. Trucks and ambulances carrying the wounded to the nearest hospital was enough evidence. As they made their way forward to join their comrades from the Army there was plenty more evidence of recent combat with dead animals scattered around in the fields, killed no doubt by stray bullets or shrapnel from exploding mortar bombs and artillery shells, houses blown to pieces, scenes you didn't see on the Newsreel in the cinema.

There were other signs of course, reports from gun and rifle fire could be clearly heard and the explosions of bombs and shells almost deafening and unending, the smell of battle, war and death was all around.

The company had arrived at the front now and the Major in charge gave a sigh of relief that reinforcement had arrived. The eastern wing of the front was very thin because most of the German forces were engaged preventing British troops reaching the isle of Corinth and from thence to be taken off by the Royal Navy to fight another day. With the company now in place and looking across Nomansland, movement by the opposition were spotted. The heart beats of the young German soldiers increased. Their throats were dry and no denying, a sense of fear came over them. "Wow," Alfred thought, being that close to action I had better keep a low profile lest I get hit by a stray bullet and end up like the animals in the meadows." Alfred was accustomed to the sound of pistols and rifles being discharged when out on the firing range for target practice but never before had he heard the sound of a bullet passing over his head. It was scary! His heart, as the hearts of the rest of the boys, was pumping faster, his knees felt as if they were buckling. Alfred's thoughts went back to the training manual. "When under attack keep a low profile and look for cover. Then when you feel the moment is right, make for it." All very well, but when is the right time when you are being bombarded unceasingly? Evidence of the wounded and lifeless bodies all round told him that many of his comrades had misjudged the moment. As for his next move, the order was very clear. Attempt to break through the enemy's line whatever the cost. An order like that could prove very costly. As the time drew near to move forward Alfred noticed that the fire from the enemy was very spasmodic and the space between the machine gun posts very wide. That could mean only one thing, that Greek and British troops were withdrawing further south to a new line. That move could mean only one thing, an attempt to delay the fall of Athens for a few days. Alfred, though daring at times, was also very careful. Just because the fire from the line opposite was light did not mean he could drop his guard and be careless. Earlier on he had spotted a large boulder that would provide him the cover he was looking for, for his leap forward, and when the command was given, went for it. He made it alright and breathed a sigh of relief. That was good news Alfred felt, darkness would soon be falling and in any case the experience of his first day ever in a live battle against an enemy of the Third Reich was enough and quite tiring too. There were scary moments it has to be said and he ducked a few times when he heard the bullets whistle past him. All in all it had been a long day for the Battalion and indeed all involved. Not that the men expected to get much sleep as they knew German artillery would continue for most of the night shelling enemy lines less than a kilometre away. They would hear the explosion of every shell and you could kiss good bye to any hoped for sleep. But then this was war and not a night exercise.

At dawn the bombardment ceased and in the distance the familiar sound of Stuka engines could be heard making sure that opposing forces would stay under cover. That would give German troops, who had been taking their places on the front line through the night, the chance to get ready to make the planned final push towards Athens in the morning. German intelligence believed the Allied line was weak at the eastern wing and hopefully an early breakthrough could be achieved. That would make it possible to take prisoners. Taking prisoners would be a bonus, denying Allied Forces well trained troops with great battle experience to take any further part in this war. That was the objective as far as Alfred understood the war game.

Sure enough, after an hour the intense bombardment from Stukas and other German bombers ceased and the hoped for final advance began, cautiously and slowly. The orders were to check every house and shed, every nook and cranny, as there may be hiding within them members of the rearguard, attempting to slow down the German advance. Alfred, being Alfred, was a bit of a risk- taker and daredevil who quite enjoyed checking out isolated huts, sheds and hiding places. Soon after midday he felt they seemed to have achieved their objective as all they encountered were Greek civilians, farmers and local peasants. This indicated to the advancing German army that British soldiers had made an orderly and disciplined withdrawal from the front line. That did not mean Alfred and the rest of the battalion could relax and let their guard down, not at all. German troops knew from bitter experience that local Greek partisans were ferocious in defending their mother country. However, no British Tommy was seen and in the afternoon they heard that Corinth had been seized by German troops and that thousands of Allied troops were trapped on the peninsular hoping in vain to be among the lucky ones to be evacuated. The Royal Navy, under constant bombardment from land and air even then, managed to rescue some 50,000 troops. However, 7,000 British soldiers fell into German hands. The day was April 26th. It was the general feeling that it would not be long before Athens fell.

Sure enough, the Parachute Pioneer Battalion along with units from other branches of the German army were told to set their sight on Athens. The final assault would begin in the morning at 07.00! Guards were doubled to nip any surprise attack in the bud. Little sleep was to be had as everybody knew that tomorrow would be the last day for some.

As expected at dawn the next day, bombers of the Luftwaffe began their short but intense bombing of the British line and at 07.00 sharp Alfred with his comrades set out once more to check out any possible hiding place where machine gunners or snipers might be hiding to slow down the German advance on the Greek capital. Unlike the day before, stronger resistance by the enemy was offered but with overwhelming odds facing the British troops it was soon realised that resistance was pointless and Alfred's platoon took their first prisoners of the war. Alfred had mixed feelings about the platoon's first scalps so to speak. Pleased that they had executed their order correctly, but also he felt sorry for his prisoners as their immediate future was unclear. How long would they have to spend behind barbed wire? A thought went through Alfred's mind, should he ever be taken prisoner how would he feel being penned in? His nature was to roam freely through fields and woods and open spaces to engage in some adventurous activity. He hoped it would never happen to him.

None of these daily advances were full frontal attacks as there was no need. Small daily gains were sufficient as British troops had nowhere to escape. The British offered just enough resistance to gain as much time as possible for an orderly withdrawal to a new defence position as well as for the Royal Navy to evacuate and rescue as many military personnel as possible to avoid another Dunkirk before the German Army took Athens. In spite of the Royal Navy's mammoth effort evacuating thousands of troops using anything afloat, German forces caught up with the British and Alfred's unit took more prisoners that day than on any other. All day long German troops rounded up thousands of British soldiers and took them to the holding compound. It was only a question of time now before Athens would capitulate, which it did later that day.

The Parachute Pioneer Battalion however were directed to make their way to Piraeus to secure the port and its installations and search for seaworthy crafts of any size and commandeer them for the German Army. Alfred and his squad went along the quay of the inner harbour, marking and recording every vessel moored alongside. Most of them were barely fit to go to sea. Any craft that was any good would have been taken by British soldiers to make their escape. Who can blame them, Alfred thought. In any case, what do we want these leaking buckets for? Alfred asked himself. Most of the vessels they commandeered were small boats, known as "Caiques" used by local fishermen with one or two small sails as well as small motor with a maximum speed of 7 knots and limited range, all of them in dire need of a coat of paint. But then, who was he to argue, time would tell what the German generals wanted them for, other than to secure them for the German Army, or to prevent any of the British soldiers hiding out somewhere and using them to escape.

Chapter 3: The British Involvement

The Greek armed forces were unable to stem the advance of the German army ever further south into the Balkans. The government in London, as well as the British Army High Command in Egypt feared, unless Greece received substantial military help it would, as the rest of the Balkans, fall into German hands and with it the possibility that many of her islands including Crete might as well. After consultation with the North African High Command in Cairo, London decided to send a Task Force to the Balkans to strengthen the hard pressed Greek forces in their effort to halt the German advance ever further south.

The Force which was assembled to be sent to help Greece included a detachment of Royal Marines many of them still in their teens, but unlike their counterparts in the German Army, British soldiers had some experience of what war was like. Italy had recently joined the war on the German side and now wanted to show Berlin that the Italian Army was as good as its German comrades. After invading Greece they also sent troops to North Africa with the quest of capturing Cairo. The government in London could not let this happen and so a counter attack was planned in which the recently arrived troops from Britain were fully engaged. Among the RMs was a young Marine, Vincent Collins by name only 18 years of age. Showing all the signs of leadership and courage and who, not surprisingly, by his heroic efforts in pushing the Italians back from where they started was promoted to Sergeant at the end of the North African campaign. Little did Vincent, or Alfred for that matter know, when they were facing each other in battle on the Greek mainland as well as on Crete, that they would, after the war, only live a few miles apart in South Hampshire after the war.

Vincent, like so many young men of his generation had volunteered for war service in the armed forces, with the preference to join the Royal Marines. Before being accepted to join any branch of the armed forces, men and women had to undergo a medical examination and other preliminaries to see whether they were fit to serve. When his call up papers came Vincent jumped for joy as he was to report to an RM training camp in Devon in a fortnight. Vincent, like so many other young men at that time being called up for War Service, organised one or two "Farewell" parties before boarding the train for Exeter from Southampton Central railway station in order to report on time for training at the Marines' camp further along the coast where training began almost at once. This was tough and very intense.

For Vincent a break from training and strict discipline at Christmas in 1939 was most welcome if brief. It was good to be home again and enjoy mother's cooking, meet some old friends and have a beer with them. Not that there were all that number of old friends around as most of them were serving King and Country in one of the armed forces, training somewhere in the UK. Back in camp after the Christmas break training was as intense as ever. There was not only the 'Know How' to learn about the weapons they were to use but also how to maintain as well as to repair them if necessary. Keeping bodily fit was also high on the agenda.

In the spring of 1940 with the rumour of an invasion of North Africa by German forces it did not come as a surprise when the company was issued with tropical kit and 10 days later boarded a troopship in Plymouth on their way to Alexandria in Egypt. With the short route to North Africa still open Italy had not yet joined the war on the Axis side so the British High Command took the opportunity to use this route to reinforce the British garrison in Egypt. This was deemed insufficient in numbers and equipment to fight the Axis forces in the deserts of North Africa and as it turned out it was just in time. Soon afterwards on June 10th 1940, Italy joined the war activating the Axis agreement signed between Germany and Italy. Not long afterwards followed the invasion of North Africa by Italian forces which opened out the war. Not surprising then that Vincent and his young and inexperienced comrades found themselves training hard in modern desert warfare day and night. The march through Libya and its occupation by the Italian forces went almost unhindered until the Allied Command felt they were ready to start a counter attack, which began in early December of that year. Vincent, as well as the rest of the Allied forces, was anxious to get going to show that the months of training had not been wasted. The first encounter with Italian forces was rather a fierce one. Casualties mounted up and Vincent realised that training for war on the firing range and the relative calm of the countryside is one thing, facing a real enemy and being fired at is quite another. Seeing tanks rolling towards you can be very frightening. In the end it is the best equipped, the best trained and most experienced force with the bravest men who will win the battle. Vincent soon realised war was not a game. However, with the British Desert Air Force superior to that of the Italians, the Allied forces soon had the enemy on the run. Good news for the government in

London but not so for Hitler in Berlin.

Many young people from Britain and most other parts of the British Empire, had their first taste of war and the devastation in its wake, and were thankful that it was no worse than it was. All the same, when rumour had it that some units may go to Greece to help their hard pushed Allies, the Greek armed forces and Resistance Fighters, against the might of the German Army the transfer, as far as Vincent and his fellow RMs were concerned could not come soon enough. The Greeks managed to hold the line against the Italian forces and even pushed them back into Albania but it was another matter facing the victorious German Army who, it seemed, no power could stop. In an attempt to stop Hitler's forces over-running Greece, as they had done in other countries in northern Europe, the British government decided to send a sizeable Task Force to the Balkans, and not too soon. Greeks were known as ferocious fighters but they lacked discipline and training in modern warfare. Equally, their weapons and other equipment were somewhat out of date so the arrival of the British was more than welcome.

Another Task Force was sent to Crete, part of that force were the RM. It did not take long for the many young soldiers of the British force to realise and appreciate that what they were facing here was a totally different might. In Africa they were chasing an army on the run but here in the Balkans they were facing a victorious army on the roll, hungry for more success. Just as well, Vincent thought, that he was fighting alongside an ally who it seemed knew no fear. The ferocity with which the Greeks attacked or counter attacked the German line was something to be experienced. It was something to be seen and believed, inspiring and infectious. There was one thing however that troubled Vincent. Witnessing how rough and cruelly the Greeks handled and treated Germans taken prisoners was almost sickening. They gave the impression they had never heard of the International Rules of War. Still, this was war and in the heat of battle, rules were broken on all sides.

The war on the Continent of Europe was more fierce than in Africa. Casualties alone were much greater, the constant attack from the air by German fighter planes was almost constant and night skirmishes quite frequent. The Luftwaffe ruled the skies. Without reinforcement on the ground there was little chance of holding the line much longer as casualties mounted daily. As expected the order for an orderly withdrawal was given and the Greeks were left to their own fate much to the surprise of many of the British soldiers.

Still, orders were orders and before long Vincent

and his fellow Marines found themselves in a little fishing harbour on the Aegean coastline waiting for sea transport, any sea transport, to take them on the short voyage across to Crete. There were countless little fishing boats tied up known locally as Caiques, from which the RN selected the most seaworthy on which to take British troops to Crete. It was hoped it could be achieved during the hours of darkness to avoid unnecessary casualties caused by air attacks which were bound to take place.

However they did not make landfall in time and as dawn was breaking Vincent told the other boys to be prepared for the worst. As predicted, soon after it was fully daylight, Messerschmitt and other fighter planes made their attack on the small flotilla of British soldiers. The boys who flew these planes were very accurate when they attacked, unlike their Italian counterparts whose attacks were disconnected and their shooting erratic. The Naval escort managed to shoot down a few but just did not have the guns on their small craft to do better. These air attacks slowed down on reaching their destination and losses of men and boats was considerable. Once land was in sight life became somewhat easier as anti-aircraft guns on shore could be brought into action. As those who survived waded ashore they were given a helping hand by soldiers of the British garrison on the island as well as local men who had joined the freedom fighters on Crete. All Vincent wanted was to get under cover and out of his wet clothes. After a few days rest those who had made it ashore were set to work building and strengthening defences in Suda Bay against a possible German seaborne invasion of Crete.

Chapter 4: The Battle of Crete

After the fall of Athens in late April 1941 and the mopping up of stray soldiers, both British and Greeks, it was back to training for the German Parachute Pioneer Battalion and intense training at that. Alfred and the rest of the camp knew the invasion of Crete was on the cards - it was just a question of when? The build up of weapons, ammunition, fuel and medical supplies, as well as field rations went on day and night. On the 18th April they knew their departure for Crete was imminent, which gave Alfred and the Battalion 24 hours grace to prepare themselves mentally for the task that lay ahead. The orders were to establish a beachhead before the scheduled drop, plus the task to give ground support to the 2nd and 3rd Para Regiments as they landed at Canea on the north side of the island.

After lunch on the 20th April the Battalion made its way down to the coast to board the fishing boats which Alfred's Company had requisitioned for use by the German army a few days earlier. Alfred's face dropped as he saw the old boats, most of them needing some repair or other. The boys were assured that the engines were all in working order as all had been serviced by army mechanics. OK, Alfred thought, we still need an element of luck to make it. At 20.00 the flotilla, which was quite substantial, set sail for Canea hoping to cover the approximately 45 Nautical Miles, in 9 hours and make landfall at 05.00 the following morning. Fortunately the weather was dry, the sea calm and some of the boys managed to get some sleep but not for long.

Soon after midnight they were awakened from their slumber by shells exploding all round them. No one told them, or mentioned, or even thought of it, that the British Royal Navy can be quite active during the hours of darkness. With no air support during the hours of darkness from the Luftwaffe, and the Kriegsmarine nowhere to be seen in the Eastern Mediterranean, the only support they had was from a few small ships of the Italian Navy which were not much help as their aimless shooting was well known. The shelling of the flotilla making its way to Crete continued on and off all night. As dawn was breaking Alfred could see the convoy had reduced greatly in numbers. With daylight on the eastern horizon, the shelling by the British Navy became more intense. A piece of shrapnel, and there were loads of it flying around, hit Alfred on his upper arm and burned him quite badly. With no medical personnel on board the only thing that could be done on the spot was to bandage the wound. With the heavy shelling from the British ships, it was not long before the boat took a hit and began to sink. Consequently the German officer in charge gave the order to abandon the boat. Swimming with heavy boots and clothing proved difficult but fortunately with the morning came help. Transport planes flying low dropped a liferaft meant for 6 people, which was soon occupied by 20 drowning soldiers fighting for survival. Others just looked for a space to get hold and clung on to the raft. Alfred observed that there were some of his comrades attempting to swim ashore, which was impossible under present circumstances as they were still some 10 Nautical Miles or more from land.

With the appearance of Stukas attacking the ships of the British Navy, life for those in the water became easier as the ships now turned their guns on the planes as they dived to release their bombs. This gave the men in the water an opportunity to make for the shore and they landed at Suda Bay where they were captured by Greek partisans who were waiting for them. With the other 20 or so survivors Alfred was taken to a British unit for interrogation by Greek personnel using treatment and methods which were not quite along the terms of the Geneva Convention, as hot water was thrown into their faces to make them talk, until a senior British officer intervened.

When Vincent saw the bedraggled German soldiers wading ashore he could not help feeling sorry for them as only 3 weeks earlier he and his comrades had found themselves in that same situation, the only difference being that when he and his surviving comrades landed in Susa Bay, they had a warm welcome. With all this preparation to fight off a German attack on Crete, Vincent, like everyone else on the Island, knew it was imminent. The question was, when? They did not have to wait too long. On the morning of 20th May 1941 all hell broke loose. After 2 hours of heavy bombing by the Luftwaffe, Vincent saw Junker 52s sweeping in low, hoping this daring approach might give the troopers a greater success establishing some hold on the ground. They already knew they would not have the support of a seaborne landing as planned. Whatever the outcome of the day, Vincent and his fellow Marines, as well as the rest of the Allied troops were ready to give them a bloody hot welcome.

The reason for the state of readiness which Allied troops were in to repel any invasion of Crete was thanks to a little gadget going by the name of ULTRA which was able to decode German messages and signals exchanged between a number of German command posts, and known only to a handful of high-ranking British officers. This enabled the Command

Headquarters of the Middle East in Cairo to keep track of German plans for the eastern end of the Mediterranean including the plans for invading Crete. This gave them time to reinforce the defence of the island by drafting in experienced British troops as well as Australian and New Zealand forces yet to be blooded in battle. What followed on that day was something Vincent had never believed could happen. In one respect he considered himself a veteran by now, having fought in two theatres of war. What greeted the German parachutists as they descended was something they had not expected. Long before they reached the ground they were attacked by Australian and New Zealand units awaiting their arrival. The German Paratroopers were really sitting ducks, unable to return the fire, hearing the bullets that missed them passing by. Many men were wounded before they reached ground, some fatally, and some fell to the ground already dead in their harnesses but those who made it were ruthless in their fighting as the final instructions were, whatever the cost, the airport must be taken and held before nightfall. The total loss of German troops did not end there. Firstly the planned beach-head by the Germans at Maleme was not as successful as hoped because the British Navy had considerable success in sinking a number of ships in the convoy carrying troops and heavy weapons, making its way to Crete. Secondly, the planned glider attack by the Germans was a total failure. The second New Zealand division placed at the western end of the Island, although inexperienced, was ready and waiting to play its part in defending the Island.

The German plan had been, as the gliders approached the landing site from the west, they would make use of a dry river bed as their landing strip. This would leave the runway at Maleme airport clear for Ju52s to land bringing much needed reinforcements as well as ammunition and heavier guns. Each man of the assault troops had only a rifle, a revolver and knife on them as they landed. Machine guns and other assault weapons were in containers dropped from supporting transport planes which the boys never saw. As the gliders came within firing range of Allied Forces on the ground they were attacked from all sides forcing many of them to crash land where they were, shot to pieces and the occupants literally annihilated. The soldiers who managed to get out of the gliders alive were confronted by the New Zealanders and engaged in fierce hand to hand fighting.

Even so, German transport planes managed to approach the airfield at Maleme but most of them were shot down and forced to crash land. It was amazing just how many pilots skilfully avoided the runway and set their planes down around the perimeter. Although German casualties were high, including high-ranking officers, nonetheless a great many troops escaped from the damaged, sometimes burning Junkers, alive if somewhat bruised and dazed. Unlike the Glider Division, the Paratroopers who landed at the parts of the airfield that were undefended were able to assemble quickly and made an advance on the New Zealand lines. The first wave of the Western Assault Regiment did much better too in as much as they at least had some support from the forces on the ground who had managed to established a Beach Head at Maleme early that morning.

Allied commanders were thankful that the day ended at it did with German troops held and confined at Maleme. Over at Canea the situation looked even more hopeful for Allied Command. The German Parachute Regiments, without any ground support, had to rely on their own skill and war experience to form some kind of presence on the ground which was not easy as over half of their comrades were either dead or lay wounded on the airfield. The back-up plan to receive reinforcement from Maleme was prevented by Allied troops. With no ground support, as it was hoped, the capture of Canea and holding it was impossible.

Their opponents were well experienced soldiers of the British armed forces, not least the small force of Royal Marines who only a few days earlier were fighting German forces on the Greek mainland. Knowing some of the tactics their enemy might employ British boys were ready to nip them in the bud. Again, the gliders which were part of the invasion did not achieve what the German Command had hoped for. Here too, German casualties were very high. By nightfall Canea was still in Allied hands and most of the German troops were Prisoners of war.

As Vincent reflected on the day's fighting he could hardly believe what he had seen and experienced that day. He had fought in two theatres of war now, North Africa and the Balkans but he had never seen such slaughter on the battle fields. With the number of German prisoners of war higher than expected, Vincent was detailed to augment the number of personnel already guarding them in what was only a temporary holding area further up the hills and more to the centre of the island. The plan was to take them even further up the mountain after the morning count. Much of the conversation among the soldiers during the night was what would the Germans attempt in the morning in their determination to capture and occupy the three main airfields in their sight, Maleme, Canea and further along the coast, Heraklion. The night was relatively quiet, and just as well, as at dawn the following day air attacks on Allied lines were resumed and two hours later another assault by troops from the 7th Air Division was attempted on the Canea airfield with much the same outcome as on the previous day. From the raised position in which Vincent found himself he could follow what was happening down on the airfield. Not for long though, after the morning count of prisoners they were organised into columns of 100 and were marched along a narrow, winding road up the mountain to a larger and more secure compound. On the way up a German prisoner with a good command of English, who came from Bavaria, said to the guards not to look too smug. He predicted they would be prisoners of the German army before too long!" Vincent just laughed, pooh-poohed the idea and did not give it another thought.

After two and a half hours of marching up the hill they arrived at their destination. How pleasant to breath in the mountain air every body thought. Much cleaner and fresher than at sea level. If there was any sleep to be had this coming night it would be more restful with the atmosphere not so oppressive. In the end, not surprisingly, little sleep was possible that following night. With no searchlights to illuminate the perimeter of the compound, guards were doubled preventing at least a mass breakout by the prisoners. That thought had already crossed Alfred Zollman's mind, not a mass break out, but rather looking for the right moment. Then take the risk and make a run for it. Alfred was used to the wide pen spaces of East Germany, countryside all around him and feeling as free as a bird in the air. The very thought of being cooped up for goodness knows how long almost depressed him. He was a gambler by nature and a risk taker, addicted card player as well. The thought of being denied all these things was very depressing. If he saw an opportunity to make a break for freedom he would take it.

The following night, whilst on duty Vincent observed, way out at sea, flashes of gunfire. The German High Command stubbornly refused to be defeated and mounted two convoys in an attempt to make a seaborne invasion. The British were alerted to this plan and a force of cruisers and destroyers intercepted the first convoy at midnight and dispersed the convoy, sinking many of the smaller boats. Again loss of life on the German side was considerable. The second convoy was intercepted in the morning. None of the boats, mainly Greek caiques, were sunk. However, no landing was attempted by the Germans.

The sea battle came not without cost to the British Navy, two cruisers and four destroyers were sunk by Stukas continually bombarding the British fleet. Having prevented a landing by German forces the Allied High Command gave a sigh of relief. To the German airborne troops on the ground it brought relief too, encouragement and hope that the battle was-turning in their favour.

Chapter 5: To-ing and Fro-ing

The German prisoners had no idea how the battle to secure ports and airfields along the western and northern coastline of Crete was progressing. They knew that masses of troops were ready to be shipped to Crete by air and sea to win the island for strategic reasons. The news they heard from fellow prisoners who were captured on the second day of battle and had joined them was not good and not very hopeful either. They were looking on helplessly from their elevated position up in the mountains and during the next 4 or 5 days observed Stukas coming and going, unloading their bombs on Allied lines, mainly troops from "down under". At night they could see the flashes of gunfire and heard the sound of explosion including the battle out at sea.

Imagine the prisoners' surprise when only 5 days later they were told by the British officer-in-command of the guard that they were free to go, but advised to stay in camp for their own safety. If they strayed out side the perimeter of the camp they would be caught by Crete's Freedom fighters, tortured and killed. Stay where you are, he emphasised once more, German soldiers would be here within the hour and take care of them. He gave a salute, made a right turn and marched out of the compound with the soldiers of the guard marching behind him.

Sure enough it was not long after that the British made their way to the appointed village to join the rest of the Allied Troops, when Alfred and the rest of the boys heard cars and trucks rumbling slowly up the winding road for a joyful reunion. After a few instructions, given by the officer-in-charge of the rescue party, the ex-prisoners mounted the transport on the way to Maleme where after a short de-briefing session they flew to Athens the following day.

All these events came rather unexpectedly to Alfred and his fellow prisoners who had resigned themselves to a long stay in the P.o.W. camp, except perhaps the chap from Bavaria who must have had some inside information and knew more than he let on.

The feverish activities at Maleme airfield, where thanks to the foresight by German pilots landing or setting down their damaged air planes around the perimeter, repairing the runway did not prove too difficult. Work had been going on all night and by the morning it was ready to be used by transport planes to land bringing in much needed reinforcement and supplies. With little or no defences either on the ground or in the air from Allied forces it was now possible to get reinforcements almost unhindered not only by air, but also by sea. With overwhelming manpower and heavy weapons at their disposal the aggressive leaders of the German invading army were now able to set out to achieve their objectives by starting to bring much needed relief to the small garrison at Canea as well as attacking Allied Troops and driving them away from costal districts starting with an attack on Galatas and so clearing the road to Canea.

It was not easy to achieve their goal as the New Zealanders offered unexpected resistance, it fell to the Maoris to slow down the German advance. They were successful for a time with their stubborn and fierce resistance. It was some of the heaviest fighting which the boys from "down under" had encountered as German fighter planes now stationed at Maleme were mounting constant strafing raids on the New Zealand line. Even so, they were not intimidated and fought several pitched battles and towards the end even hand to hand fighting to the point of the bayonet, to halt the persuing Germans from overtaking the withdrawing Allied forces. By doing so they suffered heavy losses.

****

The decision by the Allied High Command to

withdraw and evacuate all troops was not taken lightly. Although they had the troops to stage a counter-attack they lacked heavy armoury unlike the German Command. The other reason to order a withdrawal was that although the boys were ready and willing most of them were exhausted, especially the Britsh troops, who had been fighting now in three campaigns without a rest. By taking this decision they also acknowledged that the battle for Crete was lost. The plan was to start evacuating Allied troops. The Royal Navy ships reached Heraklion on the night of 28th May and managed to evacuate the garrison. From that date until 1st June the Royal Navy evacuated 18,000 men including the Maoris. Even so 12.000 men were left behind, many of them Australians. The battle of Crete lasted just 10 days.

The soldiers who were guarding the German P.o.Ws. were informed of the Allied Forces' withdrawal and to make their way to Sfakia, one of the beaches where evacuation took place. When they arrived at the place Vincent was very pleased to see his fellow Marines, but the news which they received was not good. Allied Troops assembled on the beach had not seen any ships to take them off in the previous 24 hours. So they waited and waited and after 2 days still no ships in sight. The outcome was that German troops caught up with them and as they were outnumbered the senior officer told them to surrender and Vincent recalled the words uttered by the Bavarian: "You will be <u>our</u> prisoners before long."

How quickly fortunes can change, with the tables now turned in favour of the Germans, the newly taken taken Allied prisoners had to march up and over the mountains from whence they had just come. Tired and exhausted they arrived at the purpose-built and newly erected compound divided into 4 sections each holding hundreds of prisoners with no permanent buildings within the camp, indicating to the men that it was a transit camp and before long they would be moving on. There were screened-off outside dugout toilets, and as for daily ablutions the boys were taken to a large marquee equipped with cold water taps only. As the camp was only a temporary holding it had to do; "But how long is temporary?" wondered Vincent. After a few days of these basic facilities the boys began to talk about escaping, firstly a mass breakout, which was quickly dimissed, as the chances of getting very far were nil with the island swarming with German soldiers but in the end it was decided to leave it to each individual to take a chance as and when they saw the opportunity to make a break.

Vincent saw his opportunity one day on the way

back from the daily ablution trips. The plan was that the boys would create a diversion at which moment he would make his escape and just hope he would get away with it - and he did get away with it. He knew the terrain quite well by now and the flight into the woods and up the mountain was really the easy part. The question was, what next?

Vincent's plan was to get up the mountain and as far south as he could before nightfall. With no kitchen facilities within the camp, German guards delivered meals twice a day but Vincent he had to rely on what he could find in the woods or fields and eat the fruits of the earth raw. He need not to have worried as early in the afternoon two Cretan shepherds spotted him and took him under their wings providing him with meals during the day and a hiding place at night. Goat's cheese and warm bread became one of Vincent's favourites. He stayed with the shepherds for a few days and during that time and even learned how to milk a goat. After a few days of this tense existence, on one evening when they had their meal, a Greek Orthodox priest joined them who as the evening wore on turned out to be a British agent. The agent apologised for not revealing himself earlier, no name given, as first he had to make sure that Vincent was British and not a German spy. Two days later, at evening time another knock. This time it was a Major, a member of the British Colonial Force on the Island. He had refused to surrender when the order was given, he knew what life behind barbed wire was like as he had fought in this part of the world in the 1st WW. He was in touch with the Australian High Command and they told him he would be taken off the island at dawn the following day and he looked in to say good bye and thank you to the shepherds who had been most helpful to him in every way. He wished Vincent luck for the rest of his stay on Crete.

Two days later the British agent called again. He had been in contact with the Allied headquarters in Egypt and was instructed to tell Vincent he would be take off the island just before dawn the following morning. He, the agent himself, would be back at midnight and take him to the beach himself. told on certain days in the week at a given time and arranged for Vincent to be taken off the island which happened one early morning soon afterwards. Soon after midnight the agent returned, and when Vincent had finished thanking the shepherds, their families he and the British agent made their way down the mountain to the sea shore. Once there, they did not have to wait long for the submarine to show up. As soon as Vincent was on board they got on their way, submerged and set course for Egypt and relative safety. He had a week off duty which was most welcome, so also was the food which was more to his liking, however good the goat's cheese and warm bread tasted during the time he spent with the shepherds on Crete. What Vincent enjoyed most of all was the pint of beer, it really went down well. However, the week was soon over and it was back to training as more action lay around the corner.

Chapter 6: Nice to be home again

After a brief meeting and a talk with the commanding officer of the Parachute Pioneer Battalion, Alfred with the rest of the freed prisoners boarded a train to take them back to their respective 'Home Barracks' in Germany to be told about their next engagement. After three days and nights non stop travelling, the train arrived in Standal where, at the station, Alfred and the rest of his battalion which were with him in captivity were met by military transport, which took them back to barracks where they were welcomed by the commanding officer who told them they would have a medical check-up in the afternoon and starting tomorrow would have three weeks leave, which was greeted with great vocal approval by them all. Passes and travel warrants could be collected from the office in the morning.

With such short notice there was no time to let folks back home know that he was on his way for three weeks rest and mother's home cooking. With most of the day on the train Alfred arrived at Munsterberg station late in the afternoon and as luck would have it met a local market gardener, Joseph Schneider, whom he knew quite well having worked for him on and off for a while before the war. He had come to town to put some of his produce on the train for Breslau for his cousin Till, who had a market stall in town. Till prefers the train, it gets his produce to town quickly and is still nice and fresh by the morning when it arrives. Giesdorf was only 5miles, or thereabouts, from the station so it was not very long before Alfred saw all the familiar sites and places of home. On the way Joseph told Alfred that three of his school mates had been killed in various theatres of war. That news did not surprise Alfred as he had seen hundreds of casualties in the battles of the Balkans and Crete. Joseph dropped Alfred off just a few yards from home and wished him a happy leave, saying: "Give my good wishes to Alma, I am sure she'll be over moon seeing her son looking so well." "I am sure she will," replied Alfred and thanked him for the lift and began to wonder himself what his mother would say when he rang the bell. If the truth was known, even Alfred's heart was beating a little faster. He pressed the bell and it was only moments before the door opened and there stood his kid brother Karl, mouth wide open as he could hardly believe what he was seeing, then shouting "Mama, its Alfred back from the war!" Alfred stepped into the hall, hugged his youngest brother and then his mother appeared from the kitchen with tears of joy in her eyes just managing to say: "Oh Alfred my boy it's good to see you and to know you are alive and well. You are well aren't you?" "Yes mother, apart from a little scratch from a shrapnel I received when coming ashore on Crete, I am well. In any case the wound was attended to by the British Medical Orderlies and has healed well." "By the British?" his mother replied, "Yes mother, I was a Prisoner for a few days, but about all this later. First of all let's have a decent cup of coffee." "Certainly!" His mother said, "I always keep a few beans in reserve for special occasions." Karl was bursting to ask his big brother thousands of questions but Alfred calmed him down and told him to be patient and wait till later, when they would all be together having their evening meal.

Young Karl did not have to wait too long. It was just gone 17.00 and father was usually home just after 17.30 and the family sat down for supper about 18.00. Just before Alfred's father Joseph was expected home, mother suggested that Alfred should hide in the next room and give his father as big a surprise as he had given her. Everybody agreed whole heartedly including Rudi his younger brother, who came home just before the head of the family, being equally surprised at finding his older brother at home. As the decision was unanimous there was nothing Alfred could do but get out of sight.

Right on time Werner put the key into the lock of the front door and called out: "Hi mother, I'm home, are the boys in?". "Yes!" Mother replied: "The boys are home." "Good; I'll go and take my jacket off and wash my hands and then we can have supper. I am ready for it." It took him just a minute or two before he entered the room and joined Alma and the boys for the evening meal. As he entered he saw all three standing there looking very sheepish. Hey, he thought, what have they been up to? As dozens of reasons as to why all three stood there looking rather guilty raced through his mind, he heard a familiar voice behind him saying: "Good evening papa, yes it is I, home on leave for three weeks." "My oh my, it's Alfred!" Werner said: "It is good to see you, are you well?" "He has been wounded," young Karl chipped in. "O forget it," Alfred interrupted; "It is nothing much. I shall live to fight another day." Little did Alfred know when he uttered these words that they would come true rather sooner than he had expected.

Surprise over, they all sat down to have their meal, constantly asking Alfred questions about his experience in the Balkans and on Crete. It was no secret that the plan to take the isle of Crete went terribly wrong. The family knew Alfred was involved somewhere, as the Parachute Regiment had been mentioned in the news on the radio. That mattered little now as the boy was safely home. It was a long meal as there was so much to talk about. Needless to say quite a few bottles of beer had been consumed as well as a 'schnaps' or two. It was nearly midnight before the boys stopped asking Alfred questions and let him go to bed. Exhausted as he was by now, once he was in bed, it took but seconds before he was sound asleep.

Before Alfred went to bed his mother told him he could stay in bed as long as he liked, even all day if he felt like it. She would see to it that he had his meals when he wanted them. She need not have worried, her boy did not stir all night and eventually woke up just before mid-day. Alfred admitted he needed that sleep. After he had fully woken up he felt all the better for it and went to see his mother who was in the kitchen and had started preparing the evening meal. Alma put this aside for the time being as she quickly cooked a light lunch for them both which they ate and enjoyed in each other's company. Just the two of them, which pleased her very much, under the circumstances, as she thought this might never happen again.

When eventually the two finished their meal and stopped talking, Alfred went to his room, made his bed and tidied up. That done, Alfred got on to his bike and made his way to Heidi's place. Alma had told her son that Heidi's mother would be at home as her general health was not good enough to go out to work. Wanda would be home and pleased to see and talk to him as they had not heard from Heidi since she went to Berlin right after Easter.

As Alfred knocked on the door of Heidi's home he wondered how he would find poor Wanda. As warned by his mother he found her looking rather poorly, and after listening to her story, he was not surprised. Her heart was weak and her blood pressure high. With not hearing from Heidi, her only child, and with her husband working away on war work in Dresden meaning she only ever saw him briefly at week-ends, it was not surprising that she looked and felt the way she did.

Alfred spent all the afternoon with her hoping to give her some comfort and to look to the future with confidence, especially as far as Heidi was concerned and all would be well. The bombing of Berlin made it very difficult for all the services to function as they should. Heidi's letters might easily have gone up in smoke or lay buried deep under rubble somewhere in the city. As he sat there holding Wanda's hands it struck Alfred for the first time, that not knowing of Heidi's whereabouts, also affected his own life. So far, the war actions in the Balkans and on Crete were the only things that mattered to him, self survival and getting out of it all uninjured were the only things on his mind. Now, sitting opposite Wanda he feared his hope and dream of marrying his beloved Heidi may never come true. It was with a heavy heart he said goodbye to what he had hoped would one day be his mother-in-law, and made his way home to be consoled by his dear mother who suffered personal grief during the first World War.

The thought that he may not see Heidi again stayed with him for the rest of the day. Over their evening meal Werner could see that Alfred was low in spirit, which was so unusual for him, and he needed to snap out of it. So he suggested a pint of Pilsner and a game of cards might do the trick. Alfred readily agreed and having finished their meal Alma suggested they be off and have a good time, after all half of his leave had already gone and there were only a few days left before he had to return to barracks. Going to their favourite Inn, meeting familiar faces and having a game or two of cards had the desired effect which Werner had hoped for. Alma too could see, when the men returned, that her dear son was more cheerful. Alfred's leave was soon coming to an end, he had to be back in camp not later than 18.00 Tuesday 24th July. Mother was planning a party for him that last Friday evening, inviting family and friends to come along and have a good time sending Alfred on his way with happy memories. Much of the time Alfred had left he spent with Joseph helping him to get his produce ready for the markets he was supplying.

The party Alma had arranged for Friday evening went with a swing. There was plenty to eat and drink, goodness only knows where she got it all from. After all there was a war on and after two years, shortages of everything, with the result that rationing had been introduced. No matter, every one present had a lovely time. There was one topic however that was much talked about and analysed which was the number of trains carrying heavy military armouries, making their way east towards Poland and other occupied eastern European countries. It could have nothing to do with Russia. There was a kind of "Non Aggression Pact" in operation. Besides, the trade agreement with Russia gave Germany the opportunity to buy almost unlimited amounts of grain from Russia. You could see the trains coming from the east, rumbling through the countryside, loaded with wheat, rye, barley and oats making there way west. Maybe the guns were needed as a warning to anyone who planned an uprising against the Reich somewhere down the line. Who could tell?

It was well gone midnight before the last guest left. For Alma it has been a long day but also a happy one and as she was very tired she left the clearing up till later in the morning. She was just thankful that all had gone well and everybody had a lovely time. Needless to say Alfred made the most of his last week-end at home, for the foreseeable future anyway, and did not rise till his mother called out to him that lunch would soon be ready. In the afternoon the whole family sat back, relaxed and had a snooze to catch up on lost sleep while they had the chance. After tea Werner, Alfred and Rudy went down the street to their local and had a last drink with friends old and new and a game or two of cards and then went home early for Mama to enjoy their company for a while before bedtime. There was only one more day left of Alfred's leave when all the family would be together for a while.

The Sunday turned out to be different altogether than they had planned. Just after 8 o'clock in the morning Werner woke up the whole house telling them to get up and come down and listen to the wireless. It had just been announced there would be an important announcement by the Reichsrat. All wondered what it could Maybe they would get the answer about the troop movements which had been passing through the local railway station in the last few days. They had experienced all this before of course. Even the boys could remember when such announcements were made at the time when German troops marched into the unoccupied military zone between the Rhine and the borders of France, Belgium and the Netherlands and later on when German troops occupied Bohemia or after Hitler gave the order to march into his Motherland of Austria. More recently there were such announcements with the invasion of Poland and the following Spring the beginning of military activities along the western front. Followed by the campaigns in Denmark, Norway, North Africa and more recently the battles on the Balkans and Crete in which Alfred had his first taste of war.

Here they were now, waiting patiently to learn what was happening in the world around them. Then, at 10 o'clock came the news that the German Army, supported by Germany's Allies, from Finland in the north to Bulgaria in the south, and all nations in between had invaded The Soviet Union. As in past campaigns the advance into enemy territory was swift and losses very small. Further announcements would follow throughout the day. "We've heard enough, thank you." Werner said and turned the receiver off. The family remained quiet for a while for the news to sink in. Werner and Alma had lived through the 1914-18 war, Werner fought the

Russians during that conflict, and hoped Hitler was not biting off more than he could chew. Being a fatalist Werner's philosophy was; "What will be, will be!"

Alfred on the other hand wondered where he would be sent after further training. Prior to this event it might well have been North Africa. Alma on the other hand was concerned for her three boys and what would happen to them. Being a staunch Roman Catholic she sent a silent prayer to God that this war would come to an end soon. Luckily they had had the family party on Friday as this morning's announcement might have spoiled it. With everybody in the house somewhat subdued Alfred went along to say good bye to Heidi's mum. Wanda was pleased to see him and both hoped there might be some news about, be it good or bad. As Alfred left he promised Wanda he would call in at the German central office of the Red Cross when he was in Berlin as he had two hours before his train left to take him back to his station for further training.

Back home with the family, the rest of that Sunday evening was very quiet in the Zollman's household. After their evening meal they tried to cheer each other up and played a number of board games in which they all could take part. Just before nine in the evening they packed up the games and sat around the wireless listening to the late news to hear how the fighting on the eastern front had progressed. The news was very good, the surprise attack had paid dividends as the military had hoped it would. News over, Werner turned the wireless set off and suggested that with that news they had all better go to bed and see what tomorrow would bring.

The following morning, Monday, everybody was up early to have a final word with Alfred before he left. Once the men were out of the house Alfred went to his room to get his things together and be with his mother as much as time would allow now. At the party last Friday Joseph, a family friend, had said he would be only too happy take him to the station, which was gratefully accepted by Werner and Alma. At the appointed time Joseph arrived and Alfred said the final goodbye to his mother who hugged him dearly with tears streaming from her eyes, clinging on to him as long as she could. Alfred tried to comfort her saying, "Don't cry mother, don't worry, I'll be back before you know it". After that Alfred gave his mother a final kiss turned, went out of the door and there, a few feet away, Joseph was waiting. Alfred gave his mother a last wave and they were on their way to the station just 5 miles away.

At the station they did not have to wait long. The train was on time, Alfred said good bye to Joseph, boarded the train and as it pulled out of the station waved goodbye to him thinking; "Heaven only knows when we shall see each other again. Alfred took his seat, luckily he found one, and tried to relax. Just over an hour and they would be in Berlin. He would be getting off in the centre of town, Friedrich Strasse, from where he could get to any mainline station he needed and it was also quite near the German Red Cross Centre.

Chapter 7: Back in familiar Surroundings

The journey to Berlin was uneventful and the train arrived on time even so there was considerable bomb damage all over Berlin from the previous night. As the train rolled on and came nearer the centre, more damage could be observed. Alfred got off the train at Friedrich Strasse station and went straight to the Red Cross headquarter to make inquiries about Heidi. After careful searching no trace of Heidi Funkel could be found so she was now registered in the Red Cross records as missing.

If not heartbroken, Alfred certainly left the Red Cross building with a heavy heart. All along he had carried Heidi's photo in his left side pocket close to his heart and wondered what became of her. Was she still alive with maybe just a loss of memory or was she dead and buried underneath the rubble of the many bombed and collapsed buildings in the city? He may never know what happened to her. The only consolation Alfred had was that he was not alone losing someone dear to him due to this war. All that he had to concentrate on now was to be back in his barracks by tomorrow lunch time.

Having made his way back to the railway station

with plenty of time to spare, he walked a little further along the road to one of the rest centres especially for service men in transit, to make himself comfortable and have a substantial meal. After having his papers and identity checked, Alfred went across to the dining hall looking for an empty table in a corner as he did not feel like talking to any one just at that time. He could still not get Heidi's unknown fate out of his mind as he looked very lovingly at her picture contemplating what the future would have held for them both had it not been for this war. It was not long before his meditation, reflecting what might have been, was interrupted by a sailor making his way back to his unit after a spell of leave who asked if he might join him. One of the ladies waiting at the tables served them with coffee and asked if they would be having a meal. As the answer was "Yes" she returned with a meal from the one dish menu. It was as expected, typical Army food, quite tasty and nourishing and would see them through the night. While they ate their meal the two young servicemen talked of their war experiences of which Alfred's were the greater. His table companion's service in the Kriegsmarine was limited to routine patrols in the Baltic Sea. After they had finished their meal they went across to the bar and had a large glass of beer but soon afterwards the young sailor, his home town being Stuttgart, picked up his belongings to make his way across Berlin to take the train from Stettiner Bahnhof, the station where he would board the train that would take him to Stralsund where he would pick up his patrol boat. As Alfred was not in any hurry, his train was not due to leave until 23.37, he sat back and relaxed wondering what he would find and what the training would be like after he returned to barracks. As he checked out at the Rest Centre he was handed a ration of rye bread, known commonly as Kommis Brot and a daily ration of Kunst Honig, artificial honey.

As Friedrich Strasse station was not a terminal, Alfred knew the train would not stop for very long so he had to make sure he was in good time. The weather had been cloudy but dry and continued to be so after nightfall, and just as well as that would prevent a bombing raid over night and trains would run on time. As Alfred went on to the platform he spotted five lads from his Battalion and went to join them. They had all enjoyed a happy and restful leave with family and friends but the topic they discussed was; where to next? There was a general opinion, it had to be the Russian front! As the train rolled into the station they spotted some of their comrades in the carriages as they were passing by. Obviously they had boarded the train at the terminal, thereby having a greater chance of getting a seat. No matter Alfred thought, it would not be the first time he had to stand all the way nor likely to be the last. As luck would have it there was a vacant seat in one of the compartments which he gladly took. The other occupants were two civilians, three chaps from a Tank Regiment, two sailors and himself the only one from a Parachute Regiment. The sailors were on their way to Bremen to join their ship whose name and type they did not reveal. The chatter among them soon fell silent as one by one they went to sleep. Alfred woke up just before 04.00 to answer a call of nature and when he returned to the compartment found others had begun to wake up anxious to stretch their legs. As there was yet another hour or so before they arrived at Standal he thought it was a good time to have a bite to eat. It did not take long to unpack his scarce travel ration of rye bread and artificial honey, which he offered to share with the others in the compartment. The two civilians as well as the sailors declined, but the soldiers happily accepted.

It was in the early hours of the morning the train rolled into Standal station. Alfred gathered his belongings and joined the rest of the returning Para Troopers on the platform who, like himself, were retuning from leave. Outside the station, as expected, stood a truck waiting to take them the short journey back to Gardelegen. On the way they passed the headquarters and barracks of the Parachute Regiment where they all had spent the first 6 months for their basic training after joining the Regiment before being transferred for special and unique training at Gardelegen. There was much speculation as to who would be promoted to replace those senior officers fallen or severely wounded in the battle for Crete who would later be honoured and decorated for their part in securing the island for Germany. When they arrived at the camp they were taken to their new quarters as the ones they had occupied before leaving for Crete were now taken over by the new recruits transferred from Standal for their particular special training. They were also told that evening parade would be at 17.00! There was no more to be said after that, as they all knew the drill. Sure enough, at the evening parade the officer on duty welcomed back the men that had enjoyed their well earned and deserved rest after Crete and announced that with the arrival of the new recruits the battalion was at full strength again. Orders of future training for the battalion and individuals would be posted outside the office at 09.00 the next day with an inspection of rank and file by the commanding and senior officers at 10.00! That was it for the day; the men went to the dining hall for their evening meal and then to their quarters as for the most of the veterans it had been a tiring day. Alfred was glad to lie down on his bed and stretch out. For once he did not feel like having a game or two of cards and that was rare.

Chapter 8: Preparing for the unknown

The next morning all officers and men of the Parachute Pioneer Battalion stood to attention for the inspection by their commanding officer, at the end of which he thanked the veterans who had taken part in the battle of Crete for their outstanding contribution in achieving, what seemed at one stage almost impossible, the fall of the island into German hands. At the end of the inspection the Battalion observed two minutes silence for the comrades who did not return prior to a handful of officers and men being decorated for their bravery in the campaign.

After they were dismissed Alfred and the rest of the Crete veterans crowded around the notice boards all eager to see what was coming next. What had been planned for the veterans resuming training? The most experienced were detailed to assist the NCOs with training the new recruits in hand to hand combat, others became store assistants and, in contrast, with the extended number of Para Troopers, some were sent on a catering course, whereas Alfred and one of his comrades, Horst Neuberg, whom he knew well, were to attend a four weeks driving course at the Military School of Driving somewhere in Saxony. Today was

Wednesday but they did not have to report at the Driving School until the following Monday. Alfred realised that this gave them only three more days here in camp as they had to leave on Sunday after breakfast to catch the midday train to Berlin and from there the overnight train to Dresden to make it on time. Alfred was looking for Horst when he spotted him coming across the parade ground. With the crowd around the notice board thinning out, Alfred and Horst had one more look at the board to make sure they had got it right. They would be a little wiser after they had seen the company clerk the next morning but until then they joined the rest of the Battalion and took part in the daily routine of the camp.

Next day at the given time they reported at the company's office to learn a little more about their fate. When they entered the outer office the desk Sergeant stood up and congratulated them on being promoted to Corporal, then he read them the citations, Horst's first. "Promoted for showing outstanding leadership and courage in the battle for Crete!" Next he read Alfred's citation which read: "Promoted to Corporal for showing outstanding leadership, courage and initiative in the failed seaborne landing of Crete in finding ways and means in preventing his comrades from drowning!" "Well done, both of you!" said the

Sergeant and then told them their travelling documents would be ready for collection at lunchtime the following day and dismissed them. Alfred and Horst made their way back to their quarters and started packing their few belongings, making sure that all they might need was stowed in their rucksacks. Four weeks is a long time to be away from base, so to speak. When the rest of the Platoon returned from open range training Alfred told them that Horst and himself had been promoted to Corporal, at which point the whole Platoon dropped everything they were doing and cheered whole heartedly and expressed the hope that both would return to the Battalion at the end of the driving course.

After the evening meal Alfred thought he should join his card playing companions. Playing cards was his favourite pastime after all, and get a few hands in on the next two evenings as he had no idea what his fellow students would be like, only time could tell. The next two days passed rather slowly but Sunday morning finally came and Alfred and Horst said "Good Bye!" to their closest friends before boarding the coach which would take them to the train in Standal and on to Berlin. On arrival in Berlin Alfred made his way straight to the Red Cross offices to see if there had been any news from or about Heidi. Disappointedly there was none, not that he had expected any, but human nature being what it is, one never gives up hope. However he thought that should she be found then her mother Wanda would be notified anyway. As he made his way to the Rest Centre for service men and women just a short distance away from the station to meet up with Horst he thought there was just enough time to have a coffee and a bite to eat, before it would be time to make their way to Guerlitzer Bahnhof to catch the overnight train to Dresden.

At the Rest Centre Horst was waiting for him and had kept a seat so that they could sit together till it was time to leave. As they were having their refreshments they began to speculate on what they might find at this Military Driving School and what life would be like and most importantly what would this month long course teach them. They would soon find out.

It was 06.12 when the train drew into the station at Dresden. Lots of military personnel got off the train but as far as Alfred and Horst could see they were the only two Para Troopers. How many of them were making their way to the same barracks as themselves they could not tell, however outside the station they found two trucks waiting clearly marked "Military School of Driving". At least they were expected! The Sergeant in charge told them they would not leave until 08.00

after the train from Munich had arrived which was due at 09.35. In the meantime they could go back into the station and have a coffee which was free for them and meet some of the other soldiers and ranks who would attend the same course. They did so and enjoyed talking to their fellow students, who came from every branch of the armed forces. The next hour went in a flash and after the sergeant made sure he had his full complement on board they made the 20 minutes drive to the garrison just outside the town.

As they drove past the guards through the gates they saw what none of them expected, At the far end of the parade ground under open fronted sheds nothing but motorised transport. From single motor bicycles to heavy trucks. Which one would it be for them? They soon would find out. The trucks took them to the wing that would be their home for the next 4 weeks where the Sergeant, who had met them at the station, told them their quarters would be ready and the rest of the morning was free, the mid-day meal from 12.00 and they all would meet at 14.00 sharp in the lecture room.

At the appointed hour all the 50 new arrivals had assembled in the lecture room awaiting the Sergeant and his staff. 14.00 on the dot 5 members of staff entered the room. 2 Sergeants, one of them they already met, and 3 Corporals. They introduced themselves and the subject they would be teaching. It also became clear not everyone would be taking the same course. All of them were there to learn to drive but in different classes of transport. A: Motor Bike solo; Motor Bike and side car; Light van and field car. B: Staff car and limousine; C: Heavy trucks and Goods vehicles. They would also be taught the basics of motor engines, 2 and 4 stroke, as well as minor repairs and servicing, the purpose being to keep the engine clean and running. Lectures would be at 09.00 in the morning, practical driving out on the range 14.00. The group in which they were taking part could be found on the notice board outside the office. "Oh, there is one more thing;" the senior of the two Sergeants said: "The afternoon of each Wednesday is free, well not quite. On Wednesdays, you have to attend the Sauna in groups of 10 and the time you will have to attend will be posted on the notice board on Wednesday morning. After you have been to the Sauna there is ordered a compulsory rest for the group which is strictly enforced. That is all. See you in the morning." With that the 5 Lecturers left the room. Imagine the buzz that followed: a sauna? - this must be the only military establishment in Germany providing such a facility to its men as none of the 50 assembled had come across such a facility anywhere before. "Ah well, let's go." Alfred said as he left the room: "At least here is something new to look forward to." On the way back Alfred and Horst had a look at the notice board and learned that both of them were in group A to be trained as Dispatch Riders. That is something else they had never dreamed of.

The next 4 weeks flew by. The training was thorough, detailed and tough. The Corporal who was their instructor impressed upon them time and again what mattered. What mattered most was to keep the engine working and the vehicle mobile - to keep things clean, oiled and running. To some a motor bike may just be, "a heap of iron," he suggested, "to you it is a vital weapon of war, lives may depend upon it," he kept saying. All the students agreed whatever group they were in, that the course was very instructive and most helpful. In the second half of the course Alfred's group also learned driving a motor car designed for tough terrain in case they were called upon to do so, driving lower ranking officers to staff meetings or even use it for delivering dispatches if no bike was available. All in all it was an interesting course and a lot to take on board but very, very tiring nonetheless. No wonder they had a scheduled, compulsory afternoon of rest, preceded by a sauna bath. As for being compulsory, there was no need for that as it turned out.

On the first Wednesday of the first week the men of group A assembled at 13.45 outside their quarters each with a rolled up towel under his arm to march across the square to the building in which the sauna was located getting more and more excited by the minute. The 3 attendants in charge of proceedings welcomed them and shown them into the dressing room and told them to strip bare, and when ready to proceed to the steam chamber and be seated on the wooden benches provided. As they entered the chamber they were met by hot, humid air which rather took them by surprise. When all were seated he scooped a bucketful of ice cold water from a tank and threw it over the red hot stones which immediately produced a volume of steam which opened the pores causing a vast amount of sweat to run down their bodies. After 5 minutes or so the process was repeated and the men felt their energy draining as well. When the time in the steam chamber was up they went next door to the shower room where only cold water was provided to rinse their bodies, which gave the system quite a shock for a moment or two. When all done it was back to the warm dressing room where they rubbed themselves dry, re-dressed and in orderly fashion marched back to their quarters where all of them collapsed onto their beds and instantly fell asleep waking up just in time for their evening meal. Looking back on this day in later years, Alfred recalled that just before he had dropped off to sleep, he thought what an experience this had been, how relaxed he felt in body, mind and spirit, something he would never forget, and there were 3 more visits to the sauna to come.

As the course progressed it became more exciting. So far the driving had been on made up roads in and around the garrison but in the last week it was on open range, unmade roads, lanes, tracks and uneven ground, observed by experts and experienced people to judge how the students handled their machines driving over such terrain. The last 2 days became even more exciting, for Alfred anyway. The task, to take a dispatch to a forward post last known to be as marked on the map. He was warned that once out in the open he will be spotted and shot at. The post he was to contact was under fire. To make it real, live ammunition will be used, not at him but around him, to make the exercise more realistic.

After taking possession of the dispatch Alfred gave himself a few moments to study the map and he noticed that the track passing the command centre where he was at the moment would lead to another kind of roadway that would lead him directly to the outpost he had to reach to deliver the dispatch. Alfred also noticed a number of coppices he could use for cover avoiding constant sniping. It would take a little longer to get to his destination but it would also give him a greater chance to deliver the dispatch and that he decided, was the route he would take. With the decision made he turned to the officer-in-charge, saluted and started the engine. He had a quick check to make sure the tank was full of fuel in case someone tampered with the machine and with a wave to his fellow students put the bike into gear and off he went setting out in the direction everyone expected him to take. What must have surprised everybody at the headquarters was that after only a few yards he turned off the track turning to the right and made for the nearest coppice. It was not until he had almost reached the cover of the trees that he heard rifles being discharged. By the time the riflemen aimed to fire the second round he had made it. "Well done Corporal!" were the words that greeted Alfred from the Sergeant in charge of the outpost. "You brilliantly out manoeuvred the enemy who was out to get you and the dispatch you were carrying." Needless to say Alfred was over the moon that his plan had succeeded. Later that afternoon, in a totally different part of the range, Alfred's test was to drive the staff car to a company in a forward position, preventing the enemy from making further advances. They had dug in at the outskirts of the village, using hedges and ditches as well as buildings for cover. A recent attempt by the enemy to take the village was defeated but there were a number of casualties both dead and wounded with the officer-in-charge suffering severe injuries and needing to be evacuated. That was the last message received from the unit.

With all lines of communication now down, Alfred's orders were to take the replacement for the injured officer to the village and bring back 3 of the most injured soldiers, including the officer, who needed treatment urgently. Again, Alfred had a quick look at the map and realised there was only one road, a direct route to the village, he could take. The first mile was not a problem, it was the last stretch that became tricky as the village was under constant shelling. There was also the danger of air attacks and how to dodge those. Further more, close to the village was an open stretch he had to cross which was visible to the enemy and being spotted and shot upon was a certainty. Not knowing the territory, to make his way across the fields was not on, as he was certain to encounter ditches, wet and boggy spots and sooner or later he would get stuck, becoming a target like a sitting duck, so that was out.

All this went through Alfred's mind in just a minute

or two and then, in a flash, a   picture of his childhood came into his mind recalling the hunting season in the Autumn, when he saw hares running across the open space weaving from one side to the other. That was the way he would attempt to cross that open stretch of road. It was the only option as far as he could see. Alfred went to the officer who would accompany him and told him that he was ready to go and what his plan was. He also stressed to the officer and the Lance Corporal who would ride shotgun so to speak, carrying an automatic rifle, to hold on tight when they approached the open space of the journey. As the moment came Alfred could not help but send an arrow prayer to God to be with them on this precarious journey. Yes, it was only an exercise but an exercise which had its dangers. When they came to this point Alfred went as fast as he dared, avoiding getting too near the edge of the road and slightly into the ditch and become stuck or even worse, turn the vehicle over on top of them. That was not the purpose of the exercise, but it had to be as realistic as possible, which it was. The moment they reached the open stretch explosives were set off on both sides of the road suggesting shell fire. These were scary moments for Alfred and he thought he had experienced them all when engaged in the battle of Crete only 6 months earlier. What a relief when they got through without losing an arm or leg or wheel even. "Well done Zollman" is all the officer could say. Adding: "Boy, that was scary." After a short break they made their way back to the command post were the Major in charge told Alfred he was impressed with his tactics, but even so, the car would have received several hits and in a real situation might well have had a flat tyre. But all round, commendable. To which Alfred could only reply: "Thank you Sir." That brought to an end the final day of his course at the Military School of Driving.

Chapter 9: What Next?

Saturday morning, after breakfast, the class of 50 assembled in the lecture room to officially receive the results of their tests from the Major and to obtain their driving licences all stating the group in which they had passed. With the news that everyone had completed the course successfully there was rejoicing all round. Their individual reports would go directly to regimental headquarters. "Congratulations, well done all of you!" he said and added: "Your travel documents are ready for collection from the office." And that is it Alfred thought, another chapter in my life, I was taught how to drive a car the military way.

As detailed, Alfred and Horst called at the office, picked up their papers and then made their way back to their quarters to gather their few belongings. There was nothing left to be done except to have a last look round before the truck took them to the station to take the train back to Berlin where they arrived early on Sunday morning. Looking at his watch Alfred realised that if they did not dilly-dally they could catch the earlier train to Standal and would be with their unit in Gardelegen in time for supper. "Come on Horst, let's go for it!" said Alfred and off they went and got to the station on the other side of the city.

As their return was unscheduled they had to use public transport for the last leg of their journey from the station in Standal to their garrison in Gardelegen, but even so, they got back to camp in good time for supper. Their fellow veterans greeted them warmly and were pleased to see them back. The month away seemed like a lifetime to some of them. The newly arrived recruits wondered what all this jollification was about. After the evening meal back in their quarters Alfred and Horst talked about their experience almost none stop till lights out.

Next day after morning parade they went to the office to report that they were back and to see what the future had in store for them. The company Sergeant Major welcomed them back and invited them to tell him in few words something about the course. Did they learn something from it and would they go again? The two of them told the Seageant that in general they were very impressed with the course and learned a great deal, not least how to drive. "Good;" the Sergeant said: "Now about the future. Zollman, you will remain with the Pioneer Battalion here in Gardelegen. With your experience you will help us to train the new recruits, whilst you Neuberg are being transferred to regimental headquarters in Standal as they are in need of someone like you and your newly acquired skills. Well done both of you and good luck." "Thank you Seargant." replied the two in unison, saluted and left the office. That is how the army functions and that is war.

Next morning Alfred joined the team of instructors to train the new arrivals in combat, hand to hand fighting, to be bold but not to take risks, to bond as a unit. Before this new group of Paratroopers were transferred to Gardelegen they were shown and practiced how to fold a parachute, how to jump out of an aeroplane safely and more importantly, to aim for a perfect landing without breaking any bones as an injured soldier is useless in battle. Recruits are also trained how to get out of the harness quickly and avoid becoming an obvious target. But here at Gardelegen it was all field work. Once landed they became an infantry man. Alfred had plenty of experience in that department. Although the emphasis was on preparing these 19 year old's for warfare, bodybuilding was not overlooked. The standard equipment they had to carry became quite weighty after a while. On top of that there would be occasion when cars and heavier machinery had to be moved manually which called for physical strength. Therefore body building, including route marches, were part of the training. Alfred enjoyed helping these recruits to become what they needed to be, fit for what they were called up for; ready for battle and to win the war.

The months rolled by and it was now early September. The war on the eastern front had gone well so far all along the line, from north to south, some 4000 miles or so. On the southern front advances towards reaching the oil fields in that region had gone well. In the centre, the push towards towards Moscow was relentless. The aim and hope was to get to the capital before the winter set in. On the northern end, gains were small. The objective here, it seemed to Alfred, was to prevent the Soviet Army to retake the Baltic States. It was also clear to Alfred that all along the line, troops would have to be replaced before long, but to which section would they be going? Wherever it was going to be, the Battalion was ready.

Then, unexpectedly, heavy snowfall and falling temperatures brought the arrival of an early winter and the race to take Moscow, almost in sight, ground to a halt. The troops, ready to march into the city were disappointed and the German High Command could not believe it. The weather, the unpredictable enemy, won the day. The southern wing of the line however continued its advance towards their objective, the oil fields. In Gardelegen no matter what happened anywhere else, training and physical exercises went on regardless. The battalion would know soon enough where their next engagement would be. As it happened they did not have long to wait. In the middle of October during morning parade the Colonel announced that they would be going to the eastern front replacing a parachute unit which had been up front from the day that operation "Barbarrosa" started. The Battalion's destination would be the northern wing on the Russian front. They would be based near Leningrad. All leave and day passes were cancelled as from this moment. Winter kit would be issued over the coming days. Mail would be censored. So that was it. "Might even see the Northern Lights if we are lucky," thought Alfred.

Chapter 10: The Russian Front 1

The days following the announcement of their departure to the eastern front were mostly spent queuing up. Not just queuing for winter clothing or weapons, but also for health checks including the dentist, injections and even haircuts. Time had to be found for checking that their weapons would be ready and functioning for arctic weather conditions and winter warfare including the light armoury, including the 75mm infantry field guns, which were to accompany the unit to the far north including the brand new and shining BMW which Alfred was to use as despatch rider.

A week later they learned that their departure date was to be 1st November. While all these preparations were going on Alfred wondered how he would cope with a complete change of climate in less than six months. Here he was with November fast approaching and in a week or two he would be facing arctic weather conditions while only a little while ago, back in May and June, he enjoyed the Mediterranean climate. Not to worry he thought, time will tell. There were still a few days before they left the base, and with all leave cancelled the evenings were free to enjoy a few games of cards. The feverish preparations went on right up to the day before their scheduled departure.

Long before dawn on the 1st of November, there was an early wake up call for the whole garrison as every hand was needed to load the equipment on to transport aeroplanes ready to accompany the battalion. When everything was loaded the troops boarded their allotted aircrafts and with the shout of: "Blocks away!" the planes joined the queue for take off and soon afterwards they were airborne and it did not take long before they were over the Baltic Sea. The planes kept close to the German coast to avoid entering neutral Sweden's air space. After two hours in the air they were over Lithuania and set course for an airfield near Daugavpils somewhere between Leningrad and Whitepsk. The landing was as smooth as can be expected on this much used grass runway. With not much daylight left in this region at that time of year it was vital that unloading began immediately the planes came to a halt in order to be ready and assembled when darkness fell for the journey to the front at dawn the following day. As the doors opened Alfred was hit by a blast of Arctic air that almost took his breath away but. "Just what I expected." he mumbled under his beard. With that he and the platoon made their way across the airfield to the plane that carried their equipment, including the BMW. He made sure his machine was ready to be used as he knew it would not be long before he would be called upon to take a message to someone or other on the front line. That night no one had any sleep because of the unaccustomed cold, frosty weather. It was like a non swimmer jumping into the pool at the deep end.

There was no need for the Sergeant Major to come and wake them the following morning as everybody was up and about trying to get warm. To get a really hot mug of coffee was almost impossible in these cold icy conditions. Come dawn, everyone was ready and dressed for the severe winter conditions with gloves buttoned up and face covered all but the eyes. Alfred said a quick good bye to his platoon before the company set off to take their place on the front line. He had to stay behind at the Battalion Head Quarters, which was to be his base for the duration of the battalion's employment here at the northern end of the front line.

The Regiment had taken over a large country house for their headquarter. Alfred had a room allocated to him on the top floor to share with the despatch rider attached to the Divisional headquarter, Seph by name, who proved to be most helpful. Seph impressed upon him when sent on a mission, in the early days anyway, to use the shortest marked road on the map as not knowing the terrain off the trodden footpath so to speak, could be fatal. "Leave the adventurous routes till later." Seph advised. "Thank you very much;" Alfred replied: "I will heed your advice." Then he spent the rest of the day familiarising himself with the lay out of the building and its surroundings as well as learning the names and ranks of his seniors, although he was already acquainted with some of them. He also had a very good look at the map which told him a great deal of what lay on either side of the roads he would have to travel, just in case plans might go pear shaped.

Over the evening meal Alfred and Seph had a good long chat and got to know each other quite well. Seph was two years older and had seen action in two campaigns before training as a despatch rider and was in from the start of the invasion of Russia. He had no idea why he had not been withdrawn for a rest. It was two days after Alfred's arrival when he was asked to make his first run to the front to deliver vital orders. He took Seph's advice and used the well marked route even though it took a little longer. At all the posts Alfred called on he saw familiar faces and they were pleased to see him but unfortunately there was no time to stop and chat.

As for the present situation here on the eastern front,

history had repeated itself. The Russian winter brought fighting to a stop, well not quite and not for long. The Russians may not have had the latest weapons to fight a modern war but they certainly had not lost the will to fight and defend their motherland. Shelling by guns may have been intermittent and reloading of their guns slow but they were there fighting doggedly in defence of their country all the same. Likewise the infantry, who from their defence position made daily attacks looking for a weak link in the German defences to achieve a breakthrough were not successful in find one. The German forces, the Parachute Pioneer Battalion being part of defending and holding the line, were also involved building more and stronger defences to stop the Russians breaking through and so preventing them reaching the Baltic coast. These daily assaults resulted in heavy losses on both sides, especially on the German side. Unlike the Russians, German troops were not accustomed to these harsh wintry conditions. Alfred had realised that German troops were fighting two enemies at the moment, on the one hand the Russian army, thought to be among the best, with plenty of guns, military planes, equipment and an endless supply of men to call upon if needed but they were all lacking in training in modern warfare. This would now change but takes time which might not be on their side. As for the other enemy, the severe wintry weather, that was unpredictable. No one can tell how severe it would become or how long it would last. Spring was still a long way of off!

Indeed there was Christmas to come and the New Year to be seen in. The chance of having a truce on Christmas Day and a game of football as they had on the western front in the first world war seemed most unlikely. During the last few days before Christmas fighting was very light and intermittent and ceased all together for three days. The lull in activities was most welcome by the boys of the Pioneer Battalion. Even though it was Christmas a constant and keen watch was still maintained at all times. The daily snowfall over Christmas continued relentlessly making the task of getting supplies through to the front more and more difficult. So hats off to the cooks at the Battalion's headquarter who did their best in producing a hot meal under these circumstances on Christmas Eve and surprise, surprise every one had a beer to go with it. The boys on watch along the front line were not so lucky. They had their usual stew, nourishing as it was, served in their mess tins. Back at Head Quarters to get into the mood of Christmas following the meal the assembled company sang a few hymns and carols and talked of home and the life they had left behind. Alfred's thoughts went to Heidi and he wondered what had actually happened to her. Christmas or not Alfred and his fellow despatch riders were kept busy and with the snow now six feet deep in places it made the task of getting to their destinations extremely difficult, but training, discipline and determination helped to get to where they needed to go.

No fireworks were needed to see the New Year in as the constant exchange of fire between the opposing sides made sufficient noise. There would surely be more death and destruction, pain and sorrow as a result. Days were getting longer now and small firearm exchanges were almost more constant throughout than Alfred had ever known. Extra precautions were needed now when his route took him close to the front line. Since the sun was higher in the sky every day and snow falls not as frequent and prolonged, the warmth of the sun could be felt even though it was still freezing none the less. The down side was that fighting became heavier and more prolonged by the Russians. The prisoners brought back after excursions to test the Russian defences clearly showed new and better trained soldiers as well as up-to-date arms and fighting tactics. Russian artillery too had modern guns and used heavier and more powerful shells. Frontal attacks to break through German defences continued but as before were duly repelled. That was one reason the boys were there, preventing such a thing from happening, watching day and night for any movement in the snow. With the defences being strengthened it became obvious that there were no plans for an attack on Leningrad to capture the city, but would there be a Spring offensive by the central and southern sections of the victorious German troops to march on Moscow and occupy it? Further south, would the army capture Stalingrad? These were the talking points here on the northern wing as the war continued relentlessly in 1942. After delivering the dispatches Alfred set course back to base, again using only the main road and only safe route. After reporting his return and mission successfully accomplished he had his evening meal and retired to the common room. He picked up an old magazine to read and see what life back home was like now. No doubt he missed his comrades from A company and his nightly games of cards.

Sure enough, in the new year as the days grew longer it became colder, much colder and as it turned out the coldest winter in Russia for the last 50 years. Just my luck Alfred thought and I have the misfortune to be here in northern Russia! Cold as it was fighting, mainly bombardments by both sides, continued day after day and sometimes through the night as well. The reason being for the guns not to fall victim to the severe frost conditions and become unusable. During the month of January temperatures dropped by a degree or so every night and the troops in the north had also to endure more heavy snowfalls from time to time. Gosh, Alfred thought, the training in winter warfare I had at Schliersee in 1940 to prepare me for these conditions proved totally inadequate for the conditions the troops here in the north were now experiencing.

Apart from the heavier and prolonged fighting since the new year, German soldiers had another enemy to fight, the silent killer, namely the freezing, cold Russian winter. More men died of hyperthermia or froze to death than in fighting the Russians. Equally, more men suffered frostbite or amputation of limbs than did any wounded through enemy gunfire. and Alfred saw it all as he delivered messages and dispatches all day long. He felt sorry for these boys, as many of them were under 21 years of age and lacking any kind of experience. Losses of this kind in the Russian Army were unknown, as these were the usual annual winter conditions.

Despatch riders, and Alfred among them, found that to deliver their dispatches became daily even more difficult, with snow six feet high in places making the roads more tricky to negotiate. Highways became more icy and narrower almost by the hour. These conditions changed little until the arrival of Spring and with it heavier and prolonged fighting which usually started with the bombardment. Once shelling stopped attempts were made by the Russians to break through the German lines right along the section of the Parachute Regiment. These attempts were fierce. The Para Troopers were ready and of full strength, thanks to the reinforcements which arrived at the end of February. Then as the days grew longer and with temperatures rising more serious attempts were made by the Russians to break through the German defences to recover the territory lost in the last year's invasion. These were successfully repelled by the Parachute Battalion thanks to the light field guns which the infantry had among their armoury. A 75mm gun which could be fired rapidly all day long enabled German forces to hold the line at all costs preventing the enemy from reaching the Baltic coast. That hard won ground in the last summer's fighting, was vital for the supply to German troops based at the most northern part of Norway. It was equally important for transporting vital raw materials of iron and other minerals from Norway to the factories in Germany, manufacturing weapons for their armed forces.

However, in order for the German soldiers to hold their ground proved very costly and casualties were high for both of wounded and the dead. During the lull from the first snowfall in September until now when the weather was spring like, the Russian Army modernised their weapons which were now equal to their German counterparts. Could the Parachute Battalion hold their nerve and hold their section? Yes they could and did! There were moments however when it was touch and go with a high number of casualties among the young recruits who had just finished their training and were still inexperienced in battle among the replacements. These young lads had to be watched and helped over their fright and shock as the Russians came pretty close at times when hand to hand fighting was the only way from preventing the enemy breaking through the German defences. This became almost a daily event somewhere along the line.

That was on the front line but back at the Battalion Head Quarter, Alfred had trouble of his own. Throughout the cold frosty weather Alfred had managed to keep his machine in good running order. The engine of his BMW never failed to start at the first attempt but now, with the frost, snow and melting ice the fields became boggy. Roads became almost unusable, most of them in northern Russia were not much better than tracks. With the action at the front line constant, messages about changing tactics had to reach the command posts fast. Alfred had frequently travelled these roads over the previous five months and with that photographic memory of his, could recall the sections where it might become tricky and the risk of getting stuck greater. The areas of extensive woodlands, came in very handy for cover. As always, with good preparation before going on his mission, he never failed to get the dispatches to the men they were intended for in time. With the enemy now close at hand, Alfred had to duck a few times when close to the firing line, as exploding shells nearby caused him to swerve every now and then to avoid being seriously injured. He knew from experience what it felt like when a red hot piece of iron hits you. It happened when approaching Crete by sea and under fire from the British Royal Navy. A always with these injuries you are in the wrong place at the wrong time when they happen. The red hot shrapnel that hit Alfred then entered his left arm at great speed and embedded itself in his biceps. The burning pain is almost indescribable. That was then, but Alfred had to deal with the here and now. After completing deliveries there was no time to congratulate yourself, you had to get back to headquarters in one piece where more dispatches were waiting to be delivered.

The months of March and April came and went with no let up in the fighting. In fact with more daylight hours the skirmishes seemed never-ending. Alfred, as well as the other despatch riders found the longer days helpful to them nonetheless as at least they could now see where they were going. The downside to it was that in exposed places they could also be seen by the Russians and became easy targets and with some excellent sharpshooters among the enemy needed their wits about them to avoid the bullets. Alfred was thankful more than once for the expert training he had received at the Military School of Driving and the advice given by Seph to plan his route carefully before setting out.

Then one day in early May returning from his afternoon run Alfred was called into the office where the Sergeant handed him four despatches saying: "Sorry Bieniasch there are four more despatches to be delivered, one to each of the four outposts of the Pioneer Battalion regarding actions tonight!" "Yes Sergeant!" Alfred replied, saluted, went out, jumped on his bike and off he went. On his way to the front line he just could not help wondering what these important messages were all about. But then he said to himself it is not for me to ask. He had not long to wait for answers, as on his return to Battalion Headquarters he found out. In his absence while executing his orders, a Battalion from the Parachute Regiment had arrived to replace the Pioneer Battalion during the hours of darkness. By Alfred's calculations the boys would be here by the morning waiting to be flown to a place of quiet to enjoy the rest they deserved after facing the enemy 24/7 for over six months.

Chapter 11: I do like to be beside the seaside

Tired and bedraggled the men arrived at the Battalion Headquarters where, since the staff learned that the Pioneer Battalion would be withdrawn lock, stock and barrel, everyone had worked feverishly throughout the night to have all the necessary papers ready for the flight. Hopefully they could take off as soon as the planes were ready. But where to? No-one had any idea where it might be. Some thought it may be Standal or Gardelegen, Others thought may be a holiday resort somewhere in the mountains.

However, the guessing was soon over. As they assembled on the airfield to board their planes the Colonel thanked the Battalion for holding the line, often against overwhelming odds and also against what proved to be a very hard winter. "You will all wish to know where you are headed. It is a place by the sea, the English Channel in fact to a camp near Calais in northern France. Make the most of your time whilst you have the opportunity. See you there!"

When the planes were ready the men boarded their allotted aircraft and it was once again: "Chocks away!" and take off. Four hours later they landed safely at an airfield near Calais. The boys were glad to get out and stretch their legs as sitting still for that length of time in crowded conditions was not much fun. Everyone looked forward to having a meal, followed by a night of uninterrupted sleep. However, being the military, everything was done in a disciplined and orderly fashion. Yes, they may have a fortnight free from military duties but they are still in the Army and there were just two commands they had to carry out, one, a physical check-up at the appointed time and the other to collect a new set of clothing. There would be no passes to leave the camp.

After a few days everyone began to feel more relaxed and refreshed. The amenities on site helped to restore the bodies and minds of the battle-worn soldiers. There was a pitch for ball games, parallel bars, a pommel horse and other apparatus for those interested in gymnastics. For those who liked to have a dip in the sea, not too far away was the English Channel where a strip of coastline was kept free of mines and barbed wire for about 100 metres along the beach and 50 metres out to sea, large enough to have a work-out for those who would like to. As always, ball games were the most popular activities and within days a round-robin tournament in football was organised, with the 4 Companies of the Battalion playing each other. A similar competition was played with the volley ball. To crown it all, the weather was dry, warm and sunny to help to lift the boys spirits. The rest period was extended for another week which was even more pleasing. Alfred took every opportunity to use and enjoy all that was offered to them to build up the body and mind and be ready to deal with any future task that was expected of them. What he enjoyed more than anything, as did many of his comrades, was to have a swim in the sea whenever the weather would allow them to take to the water safely. There was something else Alfred enjoyed, a game of cards every night.

Once the three weeks were over it was back to serious training for the next tours on the frontline wherever that might be. Some of the veterans may have thought that they know all there is to know what to do when in combat, but their illusions were soon shattered. While the Battalion was holding the Russians at bay, new weapons were introduced to keep up with the ever changing scene in modern warfare, and trusted weapons updated especially automatic guns, rifles and pistols. Also, rapid firing mortar guns became a helpful addition in the infantry's armoury. As the Pioneer Battalion had little experience in the field of Blitz Krieg or rapid war, it was felt now was the time to prepare the troops in case they were called upon to be part of such an unexpected and quick offensive. There was no better time than the present. The open range required for such training lay at their door. Exercises would begin in four days after the group of new recruits had settled in their quarters. These were young lads who had just finished their basic training as Paratroopers at Standal and Gardelegen and who would now complete their training in the skills required when engaged in ground fighting.

Alfred was quite happy to be out on the open range again, as delivering despatches did not require a great deal of physical exertion. In a way he looked forward to tuning up his body and being ready for any eventuality. It also gave him the opportunity to see how fit and well trained these youngsters were. He could not help thinking of Rudy and Karl, his two brothers, and how they were making out being in the armed force now. Like himself, when last he saw them they were fit and well, blooming with good health in fact. A good testimony to their mother who looked after all her men, as a loving wife and mother, to the best of her abilities.

Once out on the range the veterans soon found out how stiff their joins had became with neither space nor time to have a good workout all the time they were engaged facing the Russians. The current exercises out on the range also showed to officers and NCOs alike, the lack of fitness in these young recruits. That needed to be put right whilst under their command. and they had only a few weeks in which to achieve it. The officer in charge of training in the camp decided to use the veterans to help get these newcomers up to the standard required. Before long they would join the Regiment, they needed to be ready and fit for active involvement in any war zone they might be sent to.

Alfred thought this to be a brilliant idea, he knew that from now on any opposing force they would be facing would be well trained, disciplined and equipped. For the boys to have a greater chance of survival, physical fitness and mental alertness would be invaluable. Besides all that he thought, he would enjoy passing on his experiences in a practical way rather than just giving a talk to them. To Alfred's surprise when he took the group of 25 men allotted to him out for the first time just to see how much training they already had received, all of them revealed a great deal of military discipline, so vital for a military mission to be successful. The next day out on the firing range again Alfred was impressed in the way these young and new recruits handled their firearms confidently as well as safely and respectfully, knowing their life might depend upon it. As for taking aim and shooting at the target it was all done in the correct order, again safety being paramount and all done with military discipline.

During the mid-day break, when all of them sat in a group talking away while tucking into their "Emergency Rations," Alfred remarked how surprised he was finding such a high standard of safety in handling firearms and they told him that every teenager aged between 16 and 17 was called up now to attend a three weeks residential "Defence Awareness" course run by the Army. The syllabus also included the traditional "Square Bashing", and how to listen to a command given, then obey and execute it. Next on the list came how to handle light firearms, to keep them clean and keep them in working order ready to be used at a moment's notice. After learning about the weapons it was out to the firing range and target practice. Map reading was also included as well as how to assess distances during the day as well as by night. To look to nature around you for camouflage. "Well, it must be said, I am most impressed." said Alfred after learning of these men's training prior to being called up: "This is my promise, I will teach you as well as I can how to duck bullets when under attack and to stay alive during hand to hand combat." That is exactly what Alfred did for the next 3 months whilst his Battalion and the young recruits trained together. These field exercises and general training, including "Square Bashing," took place from Monday to Friday, but the weekend was free, well not entirely. On Saturday morning everybody did their laundry and with the warm sunshine during the summer months the washing was dry by lunch time so it could then be taken down and put away - except the trousers as they were carefully folded and laid under the mattress to be pressed. "Well," the boys said to themselves, "it is better than nothing." What Alfred enjoyed most on Saturdays and Sundays was to nip down to the beach and have a dip, weather permitting of course, which it did most of the time. There was something however that spoiled a relaxing weekend every and now and then, 24 hour guard duty. That was only to be expected, after all they were in the army now.

For relaxation at weekends, on Saturday groups of entertainers visited the camp. These could be a variety show or a small orchestra playing light music, sometimes with vocal soloists. There might also be instrumental soloists, mostly pianists it must be said, accompanied by male and female singers who rendered well known and loved songs and arias from operas. The most popular visitors to the camp however on Saturday nights were the small dance bands who played the Hit Tunes and songs of the day. There was no dancing of course as the soldiers had no female partners so to speak, neither was there a dance floor. Sunday night was Movie Night without fail and well supported. Alfred attended many of these weekend evenings but should he decide to opt out for whatever reason there was always someone available to have a game of cards with.

So the weeks and months of training relentlessly went by. Fortunately the weather was warm and mostly dry but there were the odd thunder storms as had to be expected during the summer months but whatever the weather, it never stopped their training regime. By the end of August all that needed to be taught to the young soldiers had been accomplished except for the one thing which cannot be taught, experience. They had yet to be baptised with the experience of actual battle conditions. Alfred, together with the whole Battalion, lined the perimeter of the airfield to wish them well as they took off to join the war in Russia in the last attempt by German forces to reach Moscow and to capture Stalingrad before the dreaded Russian winter arrived

A week later it was the Pioneer Battalion's turn to pack their bags and make ready to relieve their comrades on the northern wing of the battle line in

Russia. But there were still a few days to go and Alfred made the most of that time by popping down to the beach every day to have a swim. Goodness only knew when next he would have such an opportunity again. Come the winter in the east you hardly have a chance to take your clothes off and when you do, you do so as fast you can. Frost is no respecter of man. The evening before departure Alfred wrote to his mother assuring her he was well and very fit and she had nothing to worry about, at least not as far as he was concerned. Before going to bed he went along to the office and posted the letter unsealed, in the box provided.

Reveille next morning was earlier than usual, intended to allow time to leave quarters clean and tidy for the next occupants and to hand back to the appropriate departments all items that had been borrowed. There was ample time for breakfast and to collect one's kit before assembling on the parade ground and marching to the air strip.

Chapter 12: The Russian Front 2

As Calais is much further west than Standal the flight to Daugavpils took a little longer than the flight a year ago. The place itself had not changed much apart from a few additional buildings around the perimeter. As they had eaten their packed lunch on the way, on arrival at their destination it was straight out of the planes and on to the trucks which were waiting then onwards to be at the section on the front line assigned to them to hold and defend for the next 6 months or so. It was hoped they would get there before dark. This new stretch which the Battalion was to take over was further south, and also further inland, meaning that they had more land to defend. The terrain too was different. Here at the new section there were a few hills whereas the land the last time was absolutely flat. What was very noticeable, as they made their way to the front, were the woodlands, some of which were extensive and Alfred thought this could be quite a problem. He had been told he would continue as despatch rider and to remain at Battalion's Head Quarter. He looked upon these larger forest areas as a mixed blessing. On the one hand they gave more cover and protection if necessary, whilst on the other hand they also gave the enemy lots of cover to hide in should they be lucky enough to find a loophole in the German defences enabling them to attack the line from behind. That scenario had to be avoided at all cost. At the briefing before the Battalion left for the front line, they had been told much had been changed in their absence. What they needed to be aware of and look out for was that since the Spring partisans and freedom-fighters had made an appearance, making their task to defend and hold the line much more difficult. What they needed now was to have eyes in the back of their heads. No one rightly knew where these fighters came from. Were they smuggled in or had they been lying low awaiting orders from Moscow before becoming operative? What made matters worse was that among these resistance fighters were sharpshooters and these snipers certainly knew how to handle a rifle! Not only did they have good eyesight but also nerves of steel, as well as endless patience. Their background too played a great part in being selected and trained for this kind of warfare. Most likely they had come from farming stock, going out hunting with father or grandfather, knowing when and where to take cover, when to take aim and when to pull the trigger, to shoot to kill. In other words, snipers need to have a killer instinct and the war proved on all fronts that they did. There was an

105

occasion when Alfred saw for himself the proficiency of these sharpshooters. When attending lectures and briefings on the changing tactics used by the Russians on the eastern front, Alfred had heard of their skill and accuracy when choosing a target. It had become practice now, before the despatch riders were handed their orders and set off on the daily run, that they were briefed on what to look out for.

With snipers on the scene made moving along the line more difficult. Be it on foot or motorised means. Alfred still had a BMW, not the brand-new one he rode the year before, but the same model but now, since staff cars were considered to be too a big a target, all BMW motorbikes had a sidecar fitted for the use of taking commanding officers along the line for inspection of troops and defences. It was on such a day when Alfred took his Captain to inspect the front, including the most southerly point which also happened to be the post extending furthest east into Russia, that he witnessed and experienced what snipers are capable of.

After arriving at the outpost the Captain climbed up to the platform and took a good look into no-mans land then asked the soldier on duty; "How long before you are relieved Soldier!" "Within the next five minutes or so Captain." answered the soldier. "Right." Replied the Captain, "We will wait for you and you can ride pillion while we will take you back to your quarters." "Thank you, Captain." Said the guard on duty.

Whilst the Captain and the guard were talking Alfred had parked the BMW in a dip nearby using a shrub as camouflage thus making it more difficult for any roving partisans to spot him while all the time looking around, keeping his eyes open for any suspicious movement. Casting his eyes up the road he spotted a German soldier coming down the road towards the post. He called out to the Captain that the relief guard was on his way. Then suddenly all three heard the report of a rifle being fired and the man making his way towards the post kept on walking on as though nothing had happened, whilst Alfred on the other hand reacted immediately and took cover behind the shrub drawing his pistol and looking for any movement in the copse some 10 yards away but he could not detect any movement. The soldier who was on his way to take up guard duty had marched on. Why the devil does the chap not dive for cover Alfred asked himself. Suddenly after 6 or 8 paces he dropped to the ground, apparently dead. The guard, on hearing the shot being fired, instinctively swung round and in doing so released the safety catch of the machine gun ready to fire but nothing stirred on the Russian line. The Captain enquired of Alfred if he was alright and

Alfred said: "Not to worry Captain I am unharmed." The Captain told the guard he had to wait and remain on duty until a relief was sent along. Then the Captain and Alfred went to see the fallen comrade and found he had been shot right between the eyes. This was the first time for both men to witness the skill of sharp shooters, but it was not the last.

In the meantime, all the Captain and Alfred could do was to put the body in the sidecar and, with the Captain now riding pillion, they made their way back to the Battalion Head Quarters and reported what had occurred. After this traumatising experience, Alfred was excused any duties for the rest of the day. As it happened, the rest of the day remained quiet as far as any fighting was concerned but soon after dark the bombardment from the Russians began, as it did, and the German line expected fireworks in the morning.

At the Regiment's Head Quarter plans were discussed on how to deal with and counteract this new development. There was only one way; they had to fight fire with fire and train more snipers of their own. In the short term, guards were doubled but as for the future, that depended on how the war on the eastern front might develop. As expected, the following morning, true to form, frontal attacks by the Russians took place at several points along the line in the hope of finding a weak spot to break through, but as always none was found and the Russian attack was forcefully resisted and the line vigorously defended. That pattern of attack was repeated periodically. As far as Alfred knew there were no plans for an offensive on the northern wing of the front. Attempts to take Moscow and capture Stalingrad in the summer had failed, but the siege of Leningrad continued unabated.

With the arrival of October things changed quite dramatically. The month brought with it the expected and dreaded snow. It snowed almost daily, often heavy at times, and with it came another menace, the frost. How low will the temperature drop this year everybody was wondering. Those who were at the Russian front in 1941, as Alfred had been, remembered it well. No-one could do anything about the weather, what will be will be was the cry; no good worrying about it, just be prepared.

Those who had already served a term in the Barbarossa campaign and were now serving a second time also recalled how quickly after the shock of being invaded, the Russian leaders went all out to update their military hardware as well as their soldiers' training to be fit for modern warfare. The early and heavy losses of fighting men, sad as it was, were easily remedied by the almost unlimited supply of young men who could be called upon to take up arms. That modernisation of the Russian Armed Forces was felt and noted by the German High Command as it made it much more difficult to achieve their objectives including the capture of Moscow and Stalingrad.

The heavy snowfalls made it very difficult now to get around. Alfred remembered only too well the very icy conditions they had previously endured. Having a sidecar fixed to the motorbike made it that much more dangerous driving in the open as speed was greatly reduced. Knowing that partisans and sharpshooters could be encountered did not help matters either. All this set Alfred thinking. I still have my wits about me, so let's outwit them if I can by using a different route every day, delivering my despatches in a different order and leaving headquarters at different times. Yes. Alfred thought, there are different ways of avoiding being trapped and caught and that was exactly what he did, thereby avoided any disaster.

After the first snowfall there was a lull in the regular skirmishes by the Russians to test German alertness, although day and night bombardments continued there were no attempts by ground troops to test German defences Some of the more experienced veterans, when talking among themselves, wondered if the Russians had something new up their sleeves? "We'll soon find out," Alfred suggested: "Stay alert and spoil their surprise." Alfred could well recall the scenes of last year when masses of Russian soldiers made frontal attacks only to be mowed down by German machine gun fire. Attempts to use snow as camouflage were not too successful either. It was a matter of time to find out what new tactics, if any, the Russian Army would come up with this winter. They did not have to wait long to find out.

November went into December and the Pioneer Battalion spent their second Christmas on the Russian front. As far as the actual holidays were concerned, it was a repetition of the previous year. With no despatches to deliver Alfred had two days off and made the most of it. A good wash, laundering his clothes and cleaning both his weapons and his motorbike. He even found partners to have a game or two of cards with. What more can a man ask for as a Christmas present. During most of December they had frequent light snow falls. Temperatures, although they were well below 0 Centigrade, were bearable. Then just before the New Year a prolonged and heavy snowfall. Temperatures dropped noticeably. Well, well, Alfred thought, here we go again. Then one morning early in the New Year all hell broke loose.

That particular morning, Alfred had been

dispatched early to get the order of the day to the commanders on the front. At the crack of dawn he set out on his round thankful not to have to clear any snow away as the night before, though frosty, had been free from snowfall. On the way he heard the Russian artillery shells bursting, making the usual thunder rumbling noise. After the guns fell silent Alfred was listening for machine gun fire rattling away fending off any possibility of the Russians breaking through the line. He did not like the quietness, Just hearing the occasional burst from the machine gun did not seem right. Being only 2 or 3 minutes away from the last station he had to call on that morning, he could not believe what his eyes saw, hand to hand fighting. Years and years of training on what to do and how to fight in close combat instantly sprang to mind. There were no buts; his comrades were in dire need of help, he had to join the fight. Without thinking Alfred knew exactly what to do. Using your firearm in a situation was out of the question, so out came the knife and he went to the aid of an 18 year old who had his first taste of war. This young Paratrooper looked scared to death and in fact was almost at the point of death. Certainly no match for his opponent, a much older and stronger man. Alfred put his left arm around the Russian's throat attempting to pull him away from his comrade. Even the two of them had a struggle to fight off this Russian soldier. Alfred saw no alternative but to thrust his knife into the enemy's chest. Even then it was only after he administered several more stab wounds to the chest of the Russian, now fatally wounded, that he let go of the young Paratrooper. The company held in reserve for such an occasion arrived in time for the line not to give way. Looking around after events calmed down, the cost of the morning battle was clear for all to see. Alfred had not seen so many dead and wounded, on both sides, since Crete. What everybody wanted to know was, what went wrong? Yes, what indeed?

It emerged, after inspecting the battle scene, that the dead Russian soldiers wore a new design of winter camouflage for the Infantry. It was not too cumbersome and prevented the person wearing it from sinking too deep into the newly fallen snow. It was white with only part of the head appearing above the snow. In fact what the Russians were using was a new technique first thought of and developed by the Finnish Army using the snow to aid their surprise attacks. It allowed the wearer, crawling in the snow, to get to the chosen target much closer than before. Not unlike a person swimming in the water, the body being just below the surface. This became known all along the eastern front as "Snow Swimming." According to the guards reporting on the morning's battle, once the Russian Artillery stopped shelling the German line, the enemy was almost on top of them and there was no time to stop them other than hand-to-hand fighting to defend the line from being breeched. They managed it but at a cost. Later in the day when the line was inspected more thoroughly it was discovered that in two places a breakthrough had been achieved. With no-one reporting that large numbers of Russians were roaming the country side, it was assumed that there were only a handful or so, a Platoon of Commandos perhaps, who had managed to find the weak link during the height of battle, and were possibly reinforcements for the partisan fighters and there may well have been one or two sharpshooters among them. "Thank you very much," said Alfred when he heard the news; "I could well have done without that revelation. From then on the cry went watch out for those Snow Swimmers!

With the heavy losses sustained, it became very demanding for the Battalion to man and hold the line 24/7 even with the company who came to their rescue. They too suffered losses and were reduced in numbers. For the foreseeable future the line would be thinly defended. It was no good moaning about the situation as that would not change anything, it had to be done so; "Let's get on with it" was the men's attitude. Everybody just had to be more vigilant. Any worthwhile and substantial reinforcement, or even replacements, could be weeks away. Alfred was well aware that from now on his eyes needed to be everywhere. On his daily round of delivering despatches his route often went through copses or large wooded areas. On one evening, on his way to make his last delivery, darkness had already fallen and howling wolves were roaming the forest, when he came to a clearing where in the centre a group of German soldiers were warming themselves by a fire. Alfred could not believe what he saw: "What the hell do you think you are doing!" He shouted to the men. "Can't you see," they replied. "We are warming ourselves by the fire." "You stupid boys," said Alfred. He could see these young soldiers were inexperienced and could have only just finished their training and had now joined the Regiment. "These trees have eyes," he said angrily; "Have you not been told there are partisans all over place. You standing there by the fire make ideal targets for them. These Russian fighters will pick you off one by one and provide food for the hungry wolves. Now damp the fire and get the hell out of here." With that he jumped on his bike and went on his way. As he approached the clearing on his way back to base, he wondered what he might find. Just stopping for a moment he noticed the bodies of the soldiers lying on the ground, every one had had his throat cut. Alfred jumped off his bike, hurriedly tore off their identity disks thinking at least we will know who these chaps were. Then back on his bike and made off for the base as fast as he could. Rescuing their identity disks was the last thing he could do for these lads and their families.

As soon as Alfred got back to Headquarters he went straight in to the office where the Sergeant greeted him with: "You look as though you have seen a ghost Zollmann." "You might say that." Alfred answered and then told him the whole story. "You are amazing." said the sergeant after hearing the account of what happened earlier in the evening. "I'll pass this on to higher authority." With that Alfred left the office and went to lie on his bed absolutely drained of any energy and with nausea welling up within him. It was not long after this incident that rumour had it that replacements were on the way. It was not a day too soon. When the Battalion withdrew from the frontline all its members, officers included, were beginning to suffer from fatigue.

Chapter 13: Familiar Ways of Barrack Life

After a day's travelling by land and air the Battalion arrived at the Parachute Regiment's barracks at Paderborn tired and worn out. Again the Battalion was excused from taking part in any training or guard duties for the first 10 days but unlike the camp near Calais, here in Paderborn you had to look for any entertainment or light relief yourself. For the first few days after returning from the eastern front Alfred did not feel like going anywhere, nor did anyone else among the boys. They would be in Paderborn for the foreseeable future, so there was no need to take the town by storm the first weekend they were back.

After 10 days rest they fully resumed the daily routine of the barracks. It did not come as any surprise to Alfred that he was detailed to assist with the training of the newly arrived recruits. In fact he rather enjoyed passing on his knowledge to these youngsters and sharing with them his experience. As before in the camp at Calais he tried to set an example and was with them whatever the training programme of the day. For one thing Alfred felt, he needed to keep fit himself, the war was not over yet and goodness knows to which theatre of war he would next be sent. There was still fighting in North Africa. The British Eighth Army under Montgomery made enormous gains in winning back lost ground. What made it almost impossible for the German forces to halt the British advance or think of a counter attack was that the Americans had entered the war, the "German Afrika Corps" had to fight now on two fronts. So it did not come as a surprise when early in June 1943 the Battalion was kitted out with tropical gear. As before, some of the new recruits who had finished their basic training were integrated into the Battalion. These young soldiers were quite excited at the prospect of going to Africa for their first war experience. "If only they knew," Alfred thought, "war is not a game."

In any case, as he interpreted the situation from reports in the press, and taking into account the history of the war so far, German troops were about to surrender, which they did before the Battalion was ready to leave for further action. As the tropical kit was not recalled it was Alfred's guess the next tour of action would be somewhere around the Mediterranean. So it was, by the end of June that year the Pioneer Battalion of the Parachute Regiment found itself in the south of France. They flew to Avignon and then by road to a camp near Cavaillon. To Alfred's surprise it was fully equipped for training Paratroopers. There was no delay in continuing with the training. The morning sessions were given over to parachute packing over and over again, making absolutely sure everyone knew and understood how a parachute opening mechanism works. Should it not open then you only have yourself to blame. The afternoon was given over either to open range training, weapon maintenance or practising landing safely after a jump to keep bruising of the body and limbs to a minimum. That gave an indication that the Battalion would take part in a planned parachute drop. The most likely target was Sicily where the Italians were unable to prevent the 8th British/USA Division from establishing a beachhead. Once again the Parachute Regiment was sent to the rescue, as they had spent two years in the Balkans they knew what to expect after landing.

Alfred was not among the reinforcement that went to Sicily, instead he took part in intense Commando training. It had become clear, with the Americans entering the war there would be more close encounters with the enemy. American troops were trained for close combat. They also had well trained sharpshooters, with the patience of Job to make a kill. German forces had to equal that or do even better and the Paratroopers were the ideal force to be trained in this new area of warfare. There may well be undercover or secret missions to be carried out, who can tell. The Blitzkrieg was over, After a month's training, in August 1943 they were on their way to Napoli. Their flight came under attack by US fighter planes from either Tunisia or Sicily. Their aircraft suffered a number of hits which first appeared to have caused only slight damage to the wings. The plane lost altitude however but managed to keep airborne. The pilot decided to change course for Sicily which was the nearest land and attempt a landing there. When the island was sighted everybody gave a sigh of relief. With the plane flying very low, a parachute jump now impossible, the pilot decided to land in a field, but then discovered that the landing gear was damaged. To avoid a crash landing there was only one other way, a belly landing. To say that they were all scared would be an understatement. Everybody on that plan was scared to death. Alfred vividly remembered the almost countless casualties caused when German transport planes, damaged by British and troops from the British Empire, mainly from Australia and New Zealand including Maoris, defending the airport preventing an air born invasion. were forced to make emergency or crash landings on Crete. With their plane now almost touching the ground the pilot used all his skills to make a safe belly landing. Having spotted a level piece of ground he set the aircraft down perfectly, even the wings remained attached to the plane. The evacuation was a perfect text book exercise and still the aircraft neither caught fire nor exploded. Looking at the grounded aircraft, then themselves, they considered it a miracle that all of the occupants made it to safety and not one of them had even a scratch on them. After a safe time, the pilot and the NCO on board went back and scouted to see if all was well, and after a thumbs up, the rest of the platoon quickly unloaded the aircraft including the standard light field gun, a vital weapon for the paratrooper. In the meantime a staff car with a Major and his Adjutant had arrived on the scene. He quickly assessed the situation and ordered the Platoon to make their way to Paterno with haste to help the thin line there to stem the advance of US troops to give more time to evacuate German troops across the straight of Messina onto the mainland of Italy. He would organise transport for the field gun and the ammunition to be taken along. Not a bad decision Alfred thought to himself, the Battalion is rather good at keeping the enemy at bay, we proved that on our two tours on the Russian front. The Paratroopers proved their worth again in helping to delay any rapid advance by the Americans by several days. It was not easy and not without cost it must be said. The fire power of the Americans was second to none. U.S. troops were well trained and highly disciplined. Bombardment by artillery went on all night. It usually ceased at dawn and then the U.S. Air Force took over. The Paratroopers held on until told to retreat to the next line of defence. Resisting withdrawal to the last minute gave cause for many casualties both wounded and dead. Their sacrifice however enabled all the German troops to be evacuated to the Italian mainland. The Paratroopers should know, they were among the last to leave Sicily for the mainland where they were reunited with the rest of the Battalion.

Chapter 14: The Italian Campaign

After landing on the Italian mainland, for once there was no waiting to hear what to do next. The order was soon made clear. "Make your way to Salerno without delay." On arrival at the town there was a brief stop for a meal and for refuelling. All was well planned and organised and Alfred noticed as the convoy made its way to Napoli that looking down onto the beach where the Allied forces were expected to make landfall how massive and close to each other the obstacles were placed. There was very little space between the rows of defence. So, to make a quick dash for any cover by the men of the landing force was almost impossible. For Allied Troops to establish a Beach Head would prove extremely difficult and very costly both in military hardware and also human lives. It would certainly shatter the American dream of being in Rome five days after landing because they would find it hard-going to get away from the beach and further inland in order to build up a force of substantial strength to move further north.

As for the Paratroopers on their way to join the rest of the Battalion, they travelled all day before arriving at their destination. They were cheerfully greeted by their comrades who were very busy constructing a new defence line on the north side of a river running east to west with a mountain range to the north, which when completed this would become known as the Gustav Line. The party arriving from Sicily were shown to their quarters, a school requisitioned for this purpose, and were told that they had the rest of the day off, which was greeted with loud cheers.

Next morning, Alfred and his Platoon joined the rest of the Battalion to proceed with the fortification work. The hope was to delay as long as possible any rapid advance towards Rome. The defence line was sound but, it must be said, nothing like the Atlantic Wall in northern France but Alfred was pretty sure they could hold the line against the attacking Allied Army for a considerable time. The German High Command had chosen this particular spot because nature provided extra help in their delaying tactics. It was an excellent spot to erect such a defence as the surrounding terrain was mountainous and the roads were very narrow. To overcome this obstacle the Allies either had to go back to the sea, sail some 30 miles north and stage another seaborne invasion or detour 50 miles inland where again they would only find narrow, winding roads. The hills and mountains would provide little or no cover at all for them. The German High Command was well aware what would confront the Allied troops should they decide to go down this route since it was ideal terrain for laying an ambush.

The following day Alfred and two other veterans were delighted to be told that they were being given three weeks leave and deservedly so as it was well over two years since they were last at home. Next morning, the three of them were taken to the railway station in Gaeta, from where they took the train to Rome. The city was crowded with people, half of them German military personnel enjoying a short break from war. This was not in the plan of the three Paratroopers however, since their aim was to get back home as fast as possible. The best place to find out how to proceed from here was at the city's Military Headquarters where they were told to take the overnight train to Innsbruck, leaving from central station at 20.18 and with some luck they could be in Innsbruck before noon the next day which suited the three lads fine. The time to board the train could not come soon enough, and when it did come they found an empty compartment which suited the trio as they would be on that train for at least 12 hours. Most of the journey was during the hours of darkness which meant that they did not see much of the beautiful country through which they were travelling. When dawn broke they were in the Tyrol and just after 09.00 arrived in Innsbruck. Before leaving the station their papers were fleetingly checked again and following this the three of them made their way to the service men's centre for a wash, shave and breakfast. Feeling refreshed in body and mind they made enquiry as to how to proceed from here but the reply was not very satisfactory as it was suggested to them to make their way to Munich where they would find all they required regarding their onward travel - so it proved to be. They wished each other well and patiently waited for their respective trains to take them home to Stuttgart, Dortmund and to Breslau and Alfred hoped he could be home in time for supper to enjoy his mother's cooking once more as Breslau was not far away from home.

Chapter 15: Home sweet Home

As on his previous leave, there was no time to let his parents know that he was coming and hopefully one of them would be home to let him in. With all three boys now in the Armed Forces life had become rather quiet in the Zollman's household but Alfred's parents comforted themselves knowing that they were not the only family in Germany to be affected in this way.

The following day Alfred's mother let him sleep on but the smell of home-made bread drew him to the kitchen in the late morning. It certainly made a change from 2 day old rye bread, the basic standard bread issued to the troops. Whilst eating, Alfred chatted to his mother and asked about any news of Heidi but disappointingly there was none. As far as she knew, officially she was still listed as missing. Alma turned to Alfred and said: "Why don't you go and see Mrs. Funkel. I am sure she would tell you what the latest letter from the Red Cross had to say on this matter." "That is what I had in mind to do." Alfred replied, "I'll pop down to the Local and see who is still about, have a chat and a beer and then go along and see Wanda." The people in the pub were mostly elderly folk: some he knew, some he did not. It did not take long before they all sat round Alfred asking his opinion about the latest state of war down at the toe of Italy. "All I can tell you is that the troops are in good shape and in good spirit and leave it at that." replied Alfred

It was rather later than he had hoped when Alfred called at Heidi's home. Her mother was very surprised to see Alfred and at the same time overjoyed that Alfred had made the effort to come to see her. However, the news about Heidi was rather sad as the letter she had received from the Red Cross in Berlin only two days earlier stated that the file on Heidi had been closed. Officially she was still missing but presumed dead. "Well," Alfred said: "This letter does not tell us any more than we already know. All we can do is go on hoping." Deep in his heart Alfred felt sorry for Wanda because the uncertainty of Heidi's fate continued. He stayed with Wanda for a while before making his way home, thinking of the happy days Heidi and he had together. Alfred's heart was heavy when thinking of the girl he loved, not knowing her fate.

When he got home his mother was anxious to hear what the latest letter from the Red Cross contained about Heidi and how Wanda Funkel was dealing with what seemed to be their final communication on Heidi. Alfred's impression was that Mrs Funkel found it very hard to accept the fact that her only chid was dead and he said so to his mother. At 17.00 his father arrived home from work and after a delicious home cooked meal the men went to the pub for a drink and a game or two of cards. This became almost a daily routine with most of the young people having been called up to serve the war effort and many of the ladies working away from home in factories, social life and activities hardly existed. In some ways, Alfred was quite happy to have a quiet time at home during the day as there was always the evening down at the pub. That was something he missed when on active service, his nightly game of cards, because he was good at it. Alfred seldom lost a hand when playing cards, whatever the game. Maybe after all there is something in the saying: "Lucky with cards, unlucky in love!"

So the weeks flew by and all too soon Alfred started packing his few belongings to return to his unit fighting in Italy. He also checked that his pistol, rifle and gasmask were ready for use if needed. The day before he left he popped over to say goodbye to Wanda Funkel hoping his calling on her might help to her to come to terms with what was after all still inconclusive news of Heidi's whereabouts. He also made sure his transport was ready to take him to the station in the morning. He had 36 hours to get to Rome to report to the Military Headquarters there. On the last morning Alfred got up early to say goodbye to his father before he went to work. After breakfast the car called to take him to the station. His mother looked sad having to let go of her first born to go back to war, and not surprisingly shed a few tears. Little did they know at that moment as they said good bye to one another, that this would be the last time together in this house, which had been the family home for nearly 30 years.

Chapter 16: Special Duties

Alfred found the journey back to Italy tedious. Three weeks without action was enough for him and in fact he was looking forward to being back among the boys. Having travelled widely cross Europe in the last 4 years, the excitement of visiting and seeing new places had gone. Going back to Rome was just another journey in the line of duty.

After an uneventful 30 hours on the train, Alfred arrived in Rome and reported back at the Military Headquarters where he was told he was being transferred to the newly formed Paratrooper Scout Company. He would have to report back at headquarters at 08.00 next morning when, with 2 or 3 more Paratroopers, he would be taken to the training grounds in southern Italy. "That is interesting," Alfred thought, "I wonder whether I will know any of them?" It was now the end of October. The Allied invasion had taken place 6 weeks ago and the move towards Rome had not got very far thanks to the strong defences and stubborn resistance by the German forces, mainly Paratroopers. The Pioneer Battalion had moved further north to prepare a new and stronger defence line, as sooner or later Allied troops would achieve a breakthrough. British and American troops tried everything to conquer the defences, including frontal attacks. It was at a high cost of dead and wounded as well as of tanks and other armoured vehicles. The defences were sound and did not break, nor did the resilience of the German defence force. To make any progress towards Rome the Allies needed the road as well as the railway line. It was not until the German High Command decided to retreat that Allied forces commenced their march to Rome, albeit at a very slow pace. The reason was that German Infantry employed various delaying tactics helped by the terrain in which they found themselves. That was the situation as Alfred made his way to the dormitory where a bed for the night was waiting.

Next morning, 08.00 sharp, Alfred and three other Paratroopers climbed on to the lorry that would take them to Isernia, a former Italian army camp. On arrival there they registered and were shown to their quarters. Next morning the CO of the training camp introduced himself as Major Ritter and presented the other officers and NCOs in charge of training. Alfred could not help noticing that all of them wore medals awarded to them for valour on the battle field. Whatever lay ahead of them, whatever they were training for, one thing was sure they had tutors of great experience to train them who would know what they were talking about. Introduction over they learned the reason for being there. In his briefing the Major told them that they were now members of a newly formed Paratrooper/ Elite Airborne Scout Company. Their training would be tough and thorough and by the end of it they would be the best trained soldiers in any army engaged in modern warfare, including the Americans. America's new and modern ways of warfare were tested and perfected in the Far East against the Japanese and were now introduced and employed in the European theatre of war. The course would last till the end of the year and then they would be ready to go into action with the best and latest weapons at their disposal. Work began that afternoon as there was no time to lose.

Alfred had been through a few training courses but this one was going to be the toughest yet and totally different. As they left the lecture room they were handed a few notices related to the course including a time table. Alfred noticed that they were divided into groups of 10, the average size of an assault platoon, and they were to stay in that group throughout the course.

The first thing on the list was to collect the various weapons they needed on the course as well as other equipment. The boys were somewhat puzzled where all this would lead. Well they soon found out. First there was the two edged knife, sharp as a razor. Next they went to be issued with two rifles. One a rapid firing automatic rifle which could be compared to a light machine gun. The other, the latest sharp-shooting rifle, having a longer barrel thereby increasing the range of the weapon. On it was mounted the viewfinder with the best lenses ever manufactured. Finally there was the camouflage tunic, vital for any operation they might take part in. The ammunition for the sharp-shooting rifle was special too, designed to keep the sniper's hideout undetected as long as possible. With hardly any flash on firing and little or no smoke afterwards, it was ideal for this type of operation.

At 14.30 the company was together again in the lecture room where they learned in detail the functioning of the sharp-shooter rifle, how to clean it and then reassemble the weapon. They were also told about the changes in the assault rifle and how to avoid cutting themselves with the latest two-edged knife in hand to hand combat. As it turned out this course, as far as the sniper training was concerned, was designed to test the individual on how long he could remain focused on a given point such as a pillar, a door or ruins from which the enemy may emerge. It may be a stretch of open space that needed to be watched and covered to prevent anyone crossing it. The sniper has only one chance to hit the bulls eye. At the same time he needs to remain undetected because should he be spotted in his hideout the chances of getting out alive were slim.

The day was divided in three parts. Part one was an exercise for the Platoon to get as close as they could to the objective before being detected. Part two, time was spent on the firing range and part three was to defend and hold a key position at all cost with the possibility of ending with hand to hand fighting. The whole idea of repeating the exercises each and every day was to become more focused on the task at hand. For instance, in the role as a sniper the aim was to have a longer and longer period in keeping one's mind and body focused on the objective. Bullet in the breech, finger on the trigger and ready to pull when the enemy came into sight. The assault Platoon's aim was to get closer and closer to the target before being spotted by the Platoon occupying the defence post. It was done in a 'Round Robin' format. It worked well and Troopers became better at it every week. By Christmas they were ready to be employed in any operation assigned to them. The Company spent Christmas together before rejoining the troops holding, most successfully it must be said, the Gustav line. Their resistance annoyed the Allied High Command no end. Their hope to have liberated Rome by the Autumn had gone up in smoke.

Chapter 17: First Battle of Monte Casino

Since the amphibious landing at Salerno beach in early September 1943 the Allied advance towards Rome was painfully slow, as far as the Americans were concerned. Their dream of marching into Rome 5 days later was dashed because they never expected such tenacious opposition from the German Army. Establishing a Beach Head proved difficult and costly and upset their battle plan. It took 5 days to get as far as Napoli 25 miles away. Even that was by the grace of the German High Command as they controlled the war here at the southern tip of Italy. It was just south of Napoli where Allied Forces encountered the first strong defence line. Day time bombing and all night shelling did not achieve the weakening of the line as was the hope. German troops only retreated when they were ready to do so and not because they were forced to.

The new dream of being in Rome by Christmas began to fade. Three months after landing at Salerno they found themselves confronted by the Gustav line, well fortified and almost impenetrable. The line was at the foot of Monte Casino and built on the north side of a river which ran through the valley. American Generals in charge felt something needed to be done.

A Paratroop drop would not be of much help as the terrain would not lend itself to such an action and the boys would not achieve much, if anything. It was suggested that maybe another seaborne landing was needed, but where? To have maximum impact it needed to be a place north of the Gustav line. The hope was that the Germans would withdraw troops from the defence line and transfer them to the landing grounds, thereby preventing a Beach Head being established. After some discussion it was decided to make the landing at Anzio.

When the German Generals learned about this they could hardly believe what they heard. Anzio of all places! Firstly there was not much of a beach to land on and secondly the land beyond the beach was marsh land with bogs everywhere. People found it difficult to cross by foot and one needed to know where the bogs were situated as there was nowhere to seek cover if one became stuck and soldiers would become a sitting target. The German High Command agreed that this would be the case; there was no need to erect any defence barrier as nature had provided them already. Nor was there any need to withdraw great numbers of troops from other places. All that was needed, the German Generals decided, was to extend the Gustav line north along the river Sacco. That was the situation when Alfred and the newly formed company joined the front line at Monte Casino early in January 1944.

With the new invasion expected in the near future building the new defence line was set into operation immediately. This was nothing new to Alfred of course he had done it all before. In fact, German Paratroopers had become quite expert by now, in erecting strong and durable defences. Then something very unexpected happened. On the 15th &16th of March Allied bombers attacked the Monastery on top of Monte Carlo mistakenly thinking it was occupied by German troops, who in fact were dug in half way down the hill with an excellent command across the whole valley. There could be only one reason for such an instant attack, to prepare the ground for an all out frontal assault, which proved to be so. At dawn on 17th January 1944 an attempt was made to break through the Gustav line. The attempt failed because as soon as the attackers came within firing range, the soldiers were met with a hail of bullets. German Paratroopers were equipped with the latest fast firing rifles as well as machine guns which discharged more bullets per minute than ever before. In addition, the Paratroopers had the light field gun, which had proved itself in every theatre of war so far, so one couldn't find a better equipped infantry unit anywhere. The gunners targeted their shells to explode just across the river preventing anyone from even attempting to cross it. Attack over, the Gustav line proved its worth.

Later that day Alfred observed the scene and was horrified with what he saw and could not help himself saying: "O MY God, I have not seen such slaughter since Crete 4 years ago!" As the Allied medics collected their dead and wounded Alfred noticed that the majority of those carried off were British Tommies. Compared to Allied losses German casualties were light. Most of them were walking wounded which was a great relief to the German High Command. Still, this was war and one could not rest on one's laurels. Tomorrow would be another day and heaven only knows what it would bring. What did it bring? The news that the Americans had chosen Anzio after all to stage their second seaborne landing on the Italian Peninsular. The German Generals shook their heads in disbelief.

With the news of a second landing, realignment of troops urgently needed to be considered. Although fewer numbers were required to retain or even repel the landing by the Americans, which was nearly achieved, nonetheless some sections of the Gustav line might became vulnerable and Allied forces could achieve a break through. Allied Command, fully aware of

German troop movements, thought it worth trying to test the German line of defence and sent a platoon to scout out the situation. The point of the line chosen was Monte Casino railway station. The approach to the station was noticed by a lone German sentry however, who informed his Battalion Headquarters what was happening. The officer on duty relayed the message immediately to the Regimental Headquarters where the Colonel was informed of the situation and instantly summoned the Platoon of the newly formed Elite Airborne Scout Company under his command. At the briefing he told the boys of the vital importance of recapturing the station before dawn. "After securing the station you must hold it until reinforcements arrive," he stressed; "which I am organising now. What ever happens do not let the Americans settle down and strike roots. You all know the drill and tactics of how to capture a station or military post. Make sure to take plenty of ammunition and a few hand grenades which might come in useful. Off you go and don't let us waste any more time!"

During the three months training before Christmas the boys got to know each other very well and Alfred knew he could rely on receiving help and support from any of them should the need arise. Equally, the Sergeant in charge knew he could rely on his men come what may. Dawn had still not broken when the Platoon came within sight of the station which was a bonus in helping them spring into action. At the first sign of dawn the textbook action to recapture the station began. The station was surrounded by the Platoon and everybody was in his place the men having taken cover behind the various buildings around the perimeter of the station complex. The search of the outbuildings revealed they all were unoccupied, indicating that the sleepy GIs had not had the time to do so. At the sign of an unspoken signal, section by section took a leap to the nearest goods wagons, of which there were quite few about. The men were now within range for hand grenades to be used, and with no further cover between the wagons and the station building all eyes were on the Sergeant for his next command, which was the sign "hand grenades at the ready and go." At this moment a GI appeared, seeing the Paratrooper leaping towards the station he started shouting and firing at the same time but the grenades were on their way and the surprise attack paid dividends - not quite textbook style but still an advantage. The American soldiers inside the station building were able to grab their rifles and attempt to repel the invasion firing aimlessly through open doors and windows hoping to keep the invaders outside, but too late. The German Paratroopers having surrounded the station, crouching at ground level close to the platforms, out of sight from the station buildings, but equally hampered not being able to see what the GIs were up to, but hoping the Sergeant was. The men were ready for the last leap on to the platform. Every second they waited seemed like a minute, tension rising and butterflies in the tummy, hand grenades at the ready. Then after what seemed an hour, in fact were only three minutes, the Sergeant gave the signal "GO!" Over the top went the first grenades. After the last explosion over the top they went tossing the second round of hand grenades through open windows and doors into the building, and after the last explosion carefully entered the rooms and found all the GIs on the floor. A check revealed 3 of them were dead, the other 7 wounded, 2 of them rather badly. The medic in the Platoon attended to them starting with the most severely wounded. The signal man in the outfit checked the radio to make sure it was switched off and the rest went to mend the breach in the defence line and kept a lookout for the Americans who were sure to show up before too long. It was now a question who would show up first, the American relief column or the German Company of Paratroopers. As it happened it was the Germans who arrived first having had the advantage of knowing what was going on at the railway station an hour earlier than their American counterpart. After the handover of the defence post, which was what the station really was, the Airborne Scout Company returned to Headquarters taking with them the American dead and wounded. Among the German ranks no fatality but 10 wounded, 2 of them needing to be taken back on stretchers, the others were walking wounded. On their way back Alfred thought it was due to their thorough training, planning and being prepared as well as disciplined that the whole Platoon came out alive. Luck also played a part in as much that they outnumbered the opposition. Had it been the other way round, who knows, none of them may have come out alive.

After that incident, apart from minor almost daily skirmishes the front around Monte Casino was pretty quiet, partly because the Americans were struggling to establish their Beach Head at Anzio. Some American senior officers began to doubt if the landing would ever succeed. It was with sheer guts and determination that they eventually began to move inland, thanks largely to the national French Division on the northern flank. But the cost was enormous. What was lacking, compared to Salerno, was the Navy out at sea bombarding the German line.

Chapter 18: Second Battle of Monte Casino

January turned into February and up in the mountains snowfall was quite considerable and nights became colder. Temperatures dropped so rapidly that the river running through the valley froze over. At Anzio, as along all the coastline, temperatures were quite mild. With the Beach Head well established the Allied Troops at long last begin their march towards Rome. It was slow going as German Troops, well experienced in delaying tactics, defended every bend in the road to prevent a speedy march on Italy's capital, giving the German High Command more time to complete the defence line around Rome and delay the fall of Rome as long as possible. Because of this, the Allied High Command considered making another assault on Monte Casino which might tempt their German counter parts to move troops from building the defences around Rome to Monte Casino to defend the Gustav line. To test the situation, British Marines were sent to scout around and firstly look for a weak spot in the German defences. The river being frozen over would make it possible for the larger numbers of troops needed to stage an attack to get across the river more quickly, and then hopefully some of the no man's land could be occupied by Allied forces and remain in their possession. The British activities around the weak link in the line and the attempted breakthrough were spotted by an eagle-eyed German guard. and an exchange of fire took place which was brief but effective. The British Marines withdrew and as no soldier was seen, alive or dead, near the breech in the defence. it was assumed therefore that the platoon had suffered no casualties. The German officer in command of the defence line gave orders to double the guards at night and requested the Snipers to be part of the 24 hour surveillance, with Alfred being one of them. Here again, Alfred thought, the intense training will prove its worth, and it did. The German commanding officer's decision to include Snipers in the round the clock watch proved justified. A thorough inspection of the line also brought to light two more vulnerable spots. All three positions were now watched and no Allied soldier dare show his face anywhere near these weak links as no warning shots were given. The order was to wait then shoot to kill. Any Allied soldier who came into view at these closely watched three points died on the spot. So a different tactic to conquer Monte Casino was needed. The conclusion, another frontal attack.

With the newly drawn defence line now completed,

the old line half way up the mountain was abandoned and new positions taken up all along the top ridge along Monte Casino. The Gustav line was much shorter now but there were also fewer troops to defend it. Quite a number of units were withdrawn to be re-employed in the attempt to defend Rome for as long as possible, contrary to what the Allied Command had hoped. American Generals still found the stubborn resistance and the tenacious delaying tactics by the German forces irritating to say the least, both in their march on Rome as well as at Monte Casino. To make it even more irksome for the enemy, German Generals decided that in order for the new line to be as effective as possible, they would abandon the defence line halfway up the mountain - a move that must have escaped the Allied Command.

The Allied Command decided that for the second attempt to conquer Monte Casino to make an all night long bombardment along the whole length of the line and then at dawn make an all out attack and take the line at all cost. Should the attempt fail the same routine would be repeated the next day. The question was when? The heavy troop losses suffered at the first battle had not yet been fully replaced. To attempt a second attack without sufficient back up would be suicide. Most of February now became a waiting game.

British and American Generals waited for reinforcements to arrive, German Generals waited for the bombardment to commence which would signal the start of battle. It was not until late in February that the second battle of Monte Casino commenced. As the Allied troops crossed the river, which luckily for them was still frozen, and stormed up the mountain they expected to be fired upon. They were but not from the bunkers, which had become quite a feature of the landscape, but from the mountain top. From the mountain ridge German troops had an excellent view as far as the river. They were ready and waiting in their bunkers with all their firearms aimed at the recently vacated defence line. The Paratroopers light field gun ideal for mountain warfare, the mortars and machine guns, as well as every rifle were trained on the enemy.

This certainly took the attacking forces by surprise. To achieve their objective to take Monte Casino they now had to fight their way up the mountain across open space with little or no cover to crouch behind. They needed to adjust the range and direction of their guns quickly to stand any chance of taking Monte Casino. With the new targets identified and range adjusted battle commenced. Damage to the German line was considerable but still not enough to go ahead with an all out assault. When the Allied High Command realised they could not achieve their objective to take and hold Monte Casino, they ordered a retreat to give them time to take stock and work out how to proceed from there. It was well known that London and Washington wanted Monte Casino conquered. One possibility might be to occupy the old defence line vacated by the Germans and use it to their own advantage by turning the empty bunkers into machine gun nests facing the new German line. This could be done by continuously bombarding the German defences along the ridge of the mountain for 36 hours. This should be long enough to convert the bunkers for the purpose intended and at the same time move all the troops available to the front. When everything was in place the bombardment could commence beginning with a frontal assault on the mountain.

During the period of the bombardment German troops were well protected by their impenetrable defences. There were no fatally wounded in the German ranks and any soldier hit suffered only minor injuries. It was now early March and everybody knew that before long the second battle of Monte Casino would continue, which it did, rather sooner than some German officers expected. Not only that, it was more intense and fierce then was known before. Assault troops were well supported by the heavy machine gun nests now occupying the bunkers in the former German defence line causing casualties in greater numbers than expected. The 75mm Infantry Gun, a trusted friend of the men, because of its limited range proved not very effective. Casualties in the German ranks mounted, especially from bullets fired from the two machine guns nests nearest the open gap. Quick action was needed to render the bunkers and the guns useless.

Commando raids were the only answer and they had to be sooner rather than later. An urgent message was sent to the Airborne Scout Company requesting 10 men equipped for a Commando raid to reinforce the 10 already at the front. The extra men were despatched instantly and on arrival were joined by their comrades for a briefing on the raid as time was of the essence for the operation to be successful. To have the desired effect the two bunkers had to be surrounded and the men ready for action before the breaking of dawn. Fortunately the weather proved of great help. It was a new moon and overcast and the men could not have wished for anything better. Using rope ladders to get over the top, which were immediately hauled back once the last man had got away, the men made their way across territory well known to them down the slope towards the two targets. Once again endless and repetitive training paid off. Alfred of course had not only trained but also instructed new recruits in his time in the art of hand to hand combat. In fact he could almost do the raid with his eyes shut.

Back on top of the hill total silence and a sharp lookout, with the best night field glasses developed for such an occasion, was being observed. Firing to cover the retreat of the two platoons could only begin after the signal from the retreating men had been given. The German soldiers were familiar with the layout and construction of the bunkers as most of them had helped to build them, so they knew where any weak points were to be found. It was still dark when the bunkers were surrounded and every man was in place. However, the Sergeant leading the raid thought that commencing the raid whilst still dark would give them a greater effect of surprise so he gave the signal to proceed. Hand grenades ready in their hands, a second one handy to follow, pins were drawn and after a count of three they were tossed through the lookout slit followed seconds later by the second grenade tossed through the open slit by each of the men, which made it twenty in all. To break down the doors did not present any difficulty. On entering the bunker Alfred fired a short burst from his gun, warning any occupant to keep his head down. To his surprise he saw what must have been the soldier in charge of the bunker firing aimlessly and continuously up the hill towards the German line. The poor chap thought, mistakenly perhaps, that this was an all out counter attack by the Germans to regain some of the lost ground. Alfred tried to pull him away from his gun, but he held on to it like grim death, keeping the trigger pulled back and firing continuously and aimlessly towards the German line. There is only one more thing I can do Alfred thought, and in the heat of battle acting on impulse, wrenched the gun out of the Tommy's hand, forgetting it was red hot and so burned his hand very badly. Screaming and cursing he punched his opponent, who to no-one's surprise started fighting back. Only being able to fight with one arm Alfred was very much hampered and was aware he would be beaten and lose the fight unless he did something drastic and immediate. Using the injured arm and hand in fighting off the punches from his British counterpart he dragged his victim with his one good arm through the door and with his last strength lifted him high and threw him down the cliff, then lay flat on the ground for a minute to get his breath and strength back. The Sergeant noticed Alfred's last action and went across to see if he could make it back to the line. Alfred assured him that he could. Explosive charges to destroy the bunkers and render them useless for the rest of the war were laid, timers activated and the signal to retreat was given. Everybody knew that this would be the trickiest and most dangerous part of the whole operation as they would now come under crossfire, and so it turned out to be.

Again the light field gun, the friend of the German Infantry man, proved its worth. Shelling the enemies' position non stop would at least make them keep their heads down, thus preventing them shooting at the retreating handful of men. Some brave British soldiers made the attempt but never had enough time to take a good aim. Even so, some stray bullet managed to find a target in Alfred's already injured hand causing a flesh wound. His hand pained him even more now and also began to bleed. If anyone was to come out alive from this raid there was no time to stop and attend to the wound. Alfred agreed that they must carry on. They were not far from safety now anyway and thankfully some comrades jumped over the defence barrier to help the two walking wounded to make it up the rope ladder and home. Medics were waiting to give first aid and administer pain killers, then into the ambulance and off to hospital they went.

With no sign of any activities in the Allied camp during the next few days it was assumed on the German side that Allied generals had called off any major attack in the near future. Counting the cost of the attempt once again revealed that it had been a heavy price to pay in trying to break the German defence. Everybody in the German camp, from General to Private, gave a sigh of relief to see Allied troops withdraw, it gave them time now to count the cost and assess the damage. Casualties, both wounded and dead were high, but not as high as first appeared. Even so, they were considerable and so was the damage to the defences. The raid on the two bunkers the previous night was very costly. 15 of the Commandos never made it back to the line and of the remaining 5 that made it back 2 were wounded and would be out of action for a while.

For the German soldiers there was no respite after the battle. The strengthening of the line continued. The Monastery itself became almost a fortress and could withstand an awful lot of bombing and shelling. There was one section in the line however that gave great concern and this was a steep dip along the ridge which was impossible to bridge without being spotted and fired upon by the enemy. Sooner or later a further attempt by the Allies to break through the Gustav line was sure to take place. Defending this gap could prove quite a problem. If the enemy broke through there would be no way of stopping him taking the longed for

Prize. What the Allied generals might not have known was that the German high command was under orders from Adolf Hitler to defend and hold Monte Casino to the last man. Hence the urgency to find ways and means to prevent any break through at the open gap. To overcome this it was decided to build strong bunkers, one on the east slope the other one on the west slope. This would give the occupants good and commanding views of any advancing troops, both to the east as well as to the west. For the Germans the route across the gap was vital in getting ammunition and other supplies to the western section of the line unhindered. Casualties were mounting and almost reached an unacceptable level. It had almost become a lottery, you either made it or you didn't. The chance to make it across unscathed was 50/50. To do the supply run in the dark was not an alternative as the path was narrow and dropped steeply away on both sides. German Generals thought that this was the only good thing about the whole dilemma as this gap could not be taken by storming up the steep, stony mountain side because the sheer drop of the cliff side made it impossible. The loss of human lives would be out of all proportion to the enemy for the advantage gained. The German command's priority then, was to make the two bunkers as strong as possible. The two bunkers in the former defence line, now in ruins after the recent raid, helped enormously. Many of the defending troops had become quite expert in building and defending skills and tactics and knew what they had to do. They had defended and held the Gustav line for 6 or 7 weeks. They were well into March now; the days became longer and the sun warmer. With April just around the corner no-one was complaining. They were ready to fight off the next attempt whenever it came. Alfred was not complaining either.

Chapter 19: A.W.O.L.

(Absent without leave)

After a two hour exhausting and bumpy ride Alfred and the other wounded men arrived at the military hospital at Florence. After doctors had examined and assessed their injuries and wounds, they had a good shower and then were taken to their ward where Ward Sister Inge welcomed them with a warm smile and asked two of her nurses to take them to their assigned beds. Looking around Alfred noticed that his fellow patients, like himself, were not critically wounded and within days could begin their physical therapy. The burns on his hand Alfred thought, may take a little longer to heal. All in all he had got away rather lightly. If Lady Luck had forsaken him he would be dead and buried under rubble by now. Youth and good health were on his side for a reasonably quick recovery as well as being surrounded by caring people of whom Sister Inge was one. Inge took quite a shine to Alfred. Somehow she was drawn to him from the moment she met him. There was something about him that she could not find in other men. There was his sense of humour for a start, his wicked smile, as well as his caring attitude to other patients.

It was the end of March now and Spring had truly arrived. The weather was really beautiful in Italy and at that time of the year young people's fancy turns to love. Inge and Alfred were no exception. Both were now in their mid-twenties and fully mature. As Alfred was now mobile he was encouraged to take a walk in the lovely park surrounding the hospital every morning and afternoon. This became a routine whilst he stayed in hospital. In the mornings Inge always cleaned his wound, put on a fresh bandage and helped him to get dressed. After a mid-morning cup of coffee those who could walk went out to take the air chatting to each other as they strolled through the grounds. The less fortunate among them who needed a wheel chair were taken on their daily round by orderlies or nurses from the hospital. Alfred always stopped to have a word with them and so the morning simply flew by.

The afternoons were quite different. Most men went to bed after lunch and took an afternoon nap. Not so Alfred, he went out on to the terrace and waited for Inge who took her afternoon break to accompany him on his routine stroll. They went as far as the lake at the far end of the park where there were plenty of benches to sit on for a little rest. Sitting there they were holding hands, looking into each other's eyes and savouring every moment - Alfred longing to hold Inge in his arms and Inge longing to be kissed. Resistance became very difficult at times. Fraternisation was discouraged but not forbidden so in the end they accepted that just sitting together holding hands had to satisfy them for the time being.

The flesh wound on Alfred's hand healed well and quickly but the burned part took rather longer. After three weeks of excellent care and nursing Alfred was told he was fit for light duties and would be discharged from hospital to return to his unit on Friday, Alfred's unit, the Airborne Scout Company, was based at Schio at the moment. On their afternoon walk at this time Inge and Alfred were rather downhearted over the news that they would have to part the next day. On the way back from their favourite spot by the lake, Inge told Alfred she was going on three days leave tomorrow to her little bed-sitter retreat in the hills. This was the place she usually went when she had a few days off. "Why don't you come with me." she said. "We could leave early on Friday morning and spend the weekend together. On Sunday morning you return to your unit and I go back to hospital." "Impossible!" Alfred replied. "I would become a deserter." "I would not have thought so." Inge answered. "Before they realise you have gone missing and search for you, you would be on you way back." Alfred said "Not on." Inge looked at him with sad eyes and shrugged her shoulders whispering, "It would have been heavenly."

That night Alfred had no sleep. Should he take the chance and hope to get away with it or was the risk too great? It all sounded very possible and certainly was very tempting. Next morning as they made their way to the railway station the temptation became too much and he said to Inge, "I will come with you." Inge was overjoyed so went and bought the tickets and twenty minutes later they walked through the door of her little retreat home. The bed-sitter was sparsely furnished but very comfortable. Inge indicated to Alfred to sit down and relax and she would look after him during the next three days. She had managed to scrounge some coffee beans in Florence and both enjoyed having real coffee as they ate their packed lunch. Lunch over they relaxed together on the sofa and close in each others arms, were at last able to express their deep feelings for one another. Their dreams had come true! The war had taught Inge what men needed after years of separation from their wives and sweethearts. More than that, she also knew that men needed to satisfy their sexual hunger so she made this experience a memorable one for Alfred. She was aware that he had never seen a naked woman before and being 24 years old this was quite unusual for a man and Alfred could not take his eyes off her. Not surprisingly Alfred lost his virginity that day. After kissing Inge good night that evening, Alfred went across to the sofa on which he would spend the night, Inge sleeping on the one single bed. He thought "If they lock me up in the guardhouse cell for seven days on bread and water, the experience was worth it."

Where that Saturday went Alfred had no idea, all he could remember was that Sunday morning came all too soon. Still, spending two days and two nights with Inge were like days in paradise to him. They made an early start on Sunday morning and took the train back to Florence where they embraced passionately on the station platform and with a sinking feeling and aching hearts said goodbye, Inge going back to hospital, and Alfred taking the train to Bologna. As he entered the camp gate he was arrested by the guards, which he expected, and taken before the Regimental Sergeant Major. The Sergeant looked Alfred up and down and inquired very firmly: "Zollman, where the hell have you been the last two days I just informed the MP to look for you!" "I left Florence later than expected to complete my therapeutic treatment. It is a three day course intended to give complete healing of body and mind." replied Alfred. "Someone at the hospital must have forgotten to enter it on my records Sir. If you think I would desert, I can assure you that this was the last thing on my mind" "Glad to hear it, because it would have spoiled your excellent military record and your outstanding war record." said the Sergeant. "By the way, the Sergeant who led the assault on the two bunkers, rendered his report. He recommends that your action and bravery in making this mission a complete success should be recognised. As a result the High Command have awarded you The Iron Cross 1st Class." "Wow!" is all Alfred could say in reply. The Sergeant pinned Ribbon and Cross on Alfred's tunic and shook his hand saying: "Well done Zollman." The Sergeant then briefed Alfred on his next assignment. "The Battalion is expecting a company of new recruits from Gardelegen after their three months initial training. They should arrive in the morning and need to be ready in a week's time to join the front line where they will receive their baptism of fire. Their destination is Monte Casino and we cannot think of anyone more able to prepare them then you. You can tell them exactly what will confront them. Now go and have a good night's sleep. A truck leaving at 08.00 will take you to Schico where the training camp is." As Alfred made his way across the parade ground to the barracks to find a bed for the night he thought; "There beats a human heart in the body of the Regimental Sergeant Major after all." There were a number of beds available in the dormitory and Alfred selected the furthest away from the door hoping to get a good night's rest. As he turned on his side to go to sleep he thought what a heavenly week-end it had turned out to be and joyfully thought "I am no longer a Virgin Soldier."

After a good night's rest Alfred was up early, had his breakfast in the dining hall, then collected all his gear and was at the transport depot in good time to board the truck for the short journey to Schico. On his arrival he was greeted by a number of familiar faces which made quite a change. With those lads in the camp he could look forward to a game or two of cards in the evenings. It was lunch time before the newcomers turned up. With no time to lose Alfred had a session with the lads preparing for the course that lay ahead. He promised them they would be ready to do battle when they left at the end of the week. As on previous occasions Alfred went through the course with his charges to show them how things needed to be done if they wanted to stay alive for more than a day. It was a tough week and very tiring for Alfred, but he enjoyed it as he did his game of cards at the end of the day.

On schedule, the course completed, he saw the lads off on their journey to experience what war was really like. Their destination, Monte Casino. As it turned out, this company was the last reinforcement sent to the Gustav Line. After they had left, the camp felt like a ghost town but life went on much as usual. They had two days off before the next batch of recruits arrived. Alfred filled in this time doing his personal chores. Washing his clothes, having his hair cut whilst he had the chance, cleaning and polishing his boots. Once the next group arrived it would be all go again. This time however, for what ever reason, he had two weeks to knock them into shape so the pressure was not quite so great. After two weeks of hard training they all were in good shape and ready for any assignment. Their destination, to build and hold a new defence line north of Rome in order to deny the Americans and other Allied troops, once Rome had fallen, any rapid advance towards the French, Swiss and Austrian borders. Alfred also learned he was to accompany them.

Chapter 20: Third Battle of Monte Casino

With Alfred's skills and his way of training new recruits his superiors felt he would be more useful remaining in his post seeing these young soldiers through their baptism of fire, in any case repairs to the line were now completed and everybody there seemed happy and relaxed. There was even time to have a good shower and wash one's clothes, both long overdue. With the repairs finished a number of units were withdrawn to be employed in the defence of Rome. Orders to the troops at Monte Casino remained unchanged; they were to hold on at all costs. With large numbers withdrawn, that would make the task of holding the line more difficult. Numbers were down into the hundreds now.

It also came to light that the Allies had not been idle either. Making the most of moonless nights they had managed somehow to keep hold of the bunkers along the old defence line half way up the mountain. These well built defences had been turned into out-posts and were occupied by British soldiers, except the two bunkers destroyed by the Commandos a couple of months earlier. What that told the German officers was that a third attempt to attack and take the mount was being planned. From the lookout posts by the open gap, constant watch was being kept to prevent Allied soldiers getting beyond the old defence line. This, it was hoped, would prevent the enemy from laying any landmines in what was now no-man's land, in case the Germans considered a counter attack. Any movement, however small, was fired upon. If nothing else it would tell the opposing side that they were being watched. Everybody was asking himself, when will the third attempt to storm the Mount take place? Would different or even new tactics be employed? With the defences around Rome holding out so far, Monte Casino not giving an inch must have been very irritating to the Generals in command of the Allied army.

One night in the middle of May in 1944 shelling of the Gustav line by Allied artillery signalled the start of the third battle of Monte Casino and later that night bombers of the American Air Force took over dropping heavy bombs for the rest of the night. At dawn all fell quiet and after five minutes total silence. Allied troops broke cover and stormed up the hill expecting their attack to be met by heavy rifle and machine gun fire. Not so, the Gustav line appeared forsaken. The Allied High Command felt very uneasy about the lack of response by German troops and wondered what their German counterparts had up their sleeves. They were unaware that Hitler had accepted Rome would fall in the next few days and that any further sacrifice of German men in the defence of Rome would be pointless. To prevent a rapid advance north by the Americans now became the number one priority. The barriers and other obstacles on the roads out of Rome leading to Italy's northern borders with France, Switzerland and Austria were almost complete. Alfred, with other long serving Paratroopers, played a vital part in building strong and lasting defences. Again this was designed to slow down the Americans on their way north.

Unaware of all this the officers leading the attack were cautious just in case traps or mines were set. Carefully every nook and cranny as well as the ruins of the monastry were searched and nothing was found. Suddenly Paratroopers appeared waving the white flag of surrender. Again Allied officers on the spot were puzzled, unaware that it was Hitler's order for them to lay down arms. The German prisoners, as they had become now, were rounded up and taken to a quickly erected holding camp and counted. Towards the end of the day, after another thorough search, the total number of prisoners was just over 300 men. "No Wonder", a senior officer remarked, and that was all that could be said. Seeing that the defence line had withstood the night long bombing with little damage, he wondered if the Gustav line could ever have been broken.

The cost of the four months long battle of Monte Casino was high. The Allies suffered 55,000 casualties. Germany and her Axis partners losses amounted to some 20,000 casualties. Most of them were never recovered and now lie buried under the rubble of the monastery.

Chapter 21: The final Battle

Even before the fall of Rome at the end of May, the Americans found a way round the German defences north of Rome. Once they found the gap there was no stopping them on their advance north. They also had the means and know-how and the experience to blow to pieces any obstacle that stood in their way. Every barrier in the road stopped them, but never for long. Alfred in his new post since leaving hospital was very much involved in constructing these road barriers and wondered what could be done to overcome this dilemma. Alfred who had years of experience in building defences wondered what he could suggest to his commanding officer about how to overcome this problem. He thought hard but could not find an answer. The terrain was not very helpful since it was too flat to be of much help. To hold back the Americans for any length of time and delay their mission to liberate Italy completely from Mussolini's and Hitler's rule and power would mean something like the Gustav line or a well constructed barrier such as they had enjoyed in north-west Russia. To erect anything like it would take weeks and with the enemy hot on their heels the idea was discounted.

The answer to all this was an orderly retreat. For the moment all that could be done was to use as cover anything nature provided such as a dip in the ground or rock on the landscape, ditches the farmer had dug to drain his land or a hedge planted as a wind or snow break then to use small arms fire and aim at the enemy and shoot non-stop at the GIs as they searched to find a safe way through the minefield. That would slow down the advance but never stop it. The darkness of night could then be used to withdraw to new positions and prepare for the next day and use the same tactics over again. Strange at it may seem, those tactics can become very frustrating to the defence force as well as the enemy. The Americans did not take this kind of treatment without responding in kind and returned fire using mortar bombs and light field guns and were quite successful at times. German casualties mounted up day after day, the defence line became thinner almost every night. With the battlefield wide open it was not long before the Americans, using the darkness of the night, outflanked German positions and Alfred and his boys had to fight quite viciously at times to get out of this trap.

This happened once too often and this time, as they could see no other way out, the officer in charge told them to surrender. "Oh not again!" Alfred thought, but agreed with the officer's decision even though he was less experienced in war than Alfred, as indeed were most of his fellow soldiers with him. Looking at the evidence around him, surrounded by American GIs, to resist being taken prisoner with no reinforcement on the way, would have been sheer suicide. Yes, under the circumstances this was the only way to stay alive.

Alfred, who had taken a good look at the map just before the Platoon took up their positions the previous night, noticed that they were not too far away from a town called Bolzano close to the Austrian border and thought that with a little bit of luck he might find an opportunity to escape and make it into Austria. To have any chance of being successful it would have to be attempted in the next 24 hours before they were moved to a more secure camp. Alfred talked to two trusted friends about his idea in case he needed help to divert the guard's attention when he thought the moment was right to make the break. What all three men failed to notice was that one of their fellow prisoners overheard what Alfred had said to his friends. He was a strange fellow, had a mean look in his eyes and seemed to be playing up to the American guards.

Earlier in the day when the three of them strolled around the perimeter of the compound, which was not a very large one, Alfred had noticed what must have been the end of a roll of fencing wire which was only loosely attached to the post with a gap just about wide enough for him to squeeze through. After the three had passed that spot Alfred told his friends as they were walking along, in a conversational voice and manner, what he had just spotted. "Why not go for it" they replied. "I will later this evening", Alfred answered. The question was, what time and what kind of diversion would work best not to make it too obvious. As the three of them continued on their round a number of ways came to mind and were discussed. In the end Alfred suggested causing a divergence by arguing over queue jumping when they went to have an evening cup of coffee. The others decided that this was a good idea and could make it look really authentic.

When the time came for their evening coffee issue all the boys, with mugs in their hands, started queuing close to the gate where the distribution of drinks, morning and night, took place. Soon after the coffee had arrived, a little further down the line, Alfred's two friends started arguing and accusing each other of queue jumping. It was all verbal, no physical contact at all. As hoped for, all eyes were on these two arguing over such a trivial matter. The two GIs overseeing the issue of the evening drink told them to be quiet and get in line and assured them that there was enough coffee for everyone. The little storm in the tea cup was soon settled.   It took but three or four minutes, but long enough for Alfred to make his break.

All this did not go unnoticed by "Mean Look". As Alfred's two friends were arguing he was nowhere to be seen. "Mean Look" cast his eyes around the compound, which was not very large, searching for Alfred but no sign of him anywhere. Straight away he went to the guard by the gate and told him, in his broken English that one of the prisoners had escaped. The guard could not make out what this guy was driving at. A passing GI suggested calling an officer and interpreter to sort out this man's problem. Within minutes the officer with interpreter arrived and "Mean Look" told them of Alfred's escape and where he was making for. "Right," the officer said; "Take this man back to the compound and get a search party together and go after him." With darkness falling there was little hope of recapturing the prisoner before nightfall but there was always tomorrow!   Furthermore, all units had been notified of a German P.o.W. on the run.

At dawn the Platoon continued to search for Alfred who, at first light, was on his way again hoping to make good progress and with good luck reach the Austrian border the next day. The sun was still low in the sky when Alfred sensed he was being followed, an instinct he had developed during his two tours in Russia where there was always the danger of being observed or followed by someone from the local population. Alfred thought it might not be a good idea to make a run for it so the only alternative was to find somewhere to hide for an hour or two and the formation of rocks ahead of him might be the answer to his prayer. As he kept close to the rock face he noticed a crack that might be wide enough for him to get in and deep enough not to be spotted by someone passing by. What Alfred had not taken into account was the skill American soldiers have in looking for and finding their enemies. So it was that twenty minutes later the GIs looking for him spotted the crack in the rock and went across to have a closer look at it and just made out the body crouching at the end. Alfred knew then that his time of freedom was over.

A voice in perfect German called out to Alfred to come out of hiding and surrender with his arms in the air. Alfred had no choice really but to do as he was ordered. When he came out into the open the GIs searched him for weapons and told him that they admired his patriotism, but for him the war was over and he had better not try escaping again because next time he might not be so lucky. They marched him down the hill to a waiting jeep that would take him back into captivity. To Alfred's huge surprise it was not the camp from which he had escaped but a place miles away. It was not until lunch time that the jeep drew into a large Army camp by the sea. It could only be the Adriatic Alfred thought and he was pretty certain of that because he had taken note of the sun's position from the moment they had begun their journey. It was to the left of them as they set out, then gradually moved across in front of them which told him that they had been travelling south all the time. The vast extent of water he now saw could only be the Adriatic and so it proved.

It was a vast camp and Alfred was taken to a section that was fenced off by barbed wire with some 15 huts occupied by German Prisoners of War. Once inside that fenced off section a Company Sergeant Major, in charge of the camp, met him and took him inside the administration hut for registration and questioning. One question the C.S.M was anxious to have answered was: "Tell me Zollman what is the reason for you being brought to this camp all on your own? Usually new captured soldiers arrive in groups of 50 or more. Were you on your own when you surrendered?" "Not at all, there were well over 40 of us when the Lieutenant in charge told us to lay down our arms. The reason I am on my own is because I escaped from a holding compound last evening and spent the night on the run on the way to Austria, but was recaptured this morning and brought straight to this camp." "Most interesting, but before we take you to your quarters we need to take a few details to keep our records up to date." the C.S. M. said. Registration completed the Sergeant made it quite clear that he expected high standards of behaviour and discipline in his camp. German Army rules would apply at all times. As for Alfred's future, he would hear in a day or two. The C.S.M. then asked one of his orderlies to take him to hut 11 and introduce Alfred to anyone present. Not surprisingly at that time of the day there were only 5 men in the hut to whom Alfred was introduced by the orderly. The other 12 were at work somewhere within the camp's perimetre. "My word" said Alfred "This is like living in a luxurious holiday camp somewhere by the sea. Somewhat different to my first experience when I was taken prisoner on Crete 3 years ago." When the boys heard that he had taken part in the invasion of Crete and became a P.o.W. they asked Alfred a lot of questions but he declined and told them he would tell them another time. For one thing it was lunch time and he had not eaten a great deal in the last 48 hours. Just talking of food made him feel hungry and he also was looking forward to having a bite to eat. What's more he would like to lay on his bed and have some shut-eye. The boys understood that and all 6 went across to the dining hut where a light meal was being served for those in camp. That in itself made Alfred feel better and back in the hut it did not take long before he was sound asleep.

A lot of talk and laughter aroused Alfred from his sleep and looking at the clock over the entrance door he found that it had just gone 5 pm. So he had enjoyed three hours refreshing sleep, and that too was a luxury. As the minutes ticked by more lads arrived and Alfred learned that most of the working gangs within the camp perimeter finished in time to be back in the enclosure set aside for P.o.Ws by 5 pm. Unavoidably a queue formed outside the main gate as everybody was searched for weapons and contraband such as alcohol or stolen goods items which may have been taken from any of the warehouses in which the boys were working. But it must be said, everybody was back by 5.30 and on the parade ground for the evening count. By 6 pm everybody had washed and shaved and were making their way to the dining hut. Meal over and back in the their hut it didn't take long for Alfred to spot some of the boys playing cards. Alfred felt that this was all he needed to make him feel at home and before long he played his first game of cards, something he passionately loved but almost became his undoing.

Chapter 22: On the Shore of the Adriatic

The following morning with most of the boys out to work, the camp was almost deserted and not being in any hurry Alfred gave everybody priority in the wash room and was last in the queue for breakfast. After he had made his bed and swept the floor of the hut, he took a stroll around the camp to make himself familiar with all the public and official buildings. There was only one official building with which he was already acquainted. In one half all the offices were located and in the other half was the first aid post, more like a Cottage Hospital. It had a consulting room in which the American Army Doctor on duty could be seen and consulted. The office hours were 0600-0900 and 1800-2100 Monday to Friday. Any minor injuries during the day were dealt with by one of the two German Army Medics. Emergency cases over the weekend were taken by ambulance to the Army Hospital within the Army compound.

There were 4 public buildings, one of which he had already been in, the dining hall of course. One of the other buildings was set aside for games rooms. Next to this was the laundry and then there was the canteen located next to the dining hall. It would be quite a while before Alfred could visit the canteen as he would have to earn some money first since he had not even started work duties and after that he would have to wait a month before the first pay day quite along time. Once he started work, would get 80 cents a day for his labours. That would come to $18.20 a month. "Now that is something to look forward to;" said Alfred when he learned he was being paid for his labours.

On the way back to his hut he was called into the office where the Sergeant told him he would start work the following day as a Steward in the Officers Club at Bari Harbour, just outside Rimini some 5 miles or so from the camp. It would be shift work and details concerning the kind of work and the shift pattern would be explained to him at the Club when he got there. All he needed to know at the moment was to be at the main gate at 09.30 in the morning. On the way back to his quarters Alfred wondered what kind of a job he had landed. He would ask around among the boys this evening to see if any one could enlighten him. They could certainly tell him what the job entailed. He found out it was to act as waiter during meal times, and steward in the lounges at any other time. He would also be responsible for keeping all the ground floor rooms, including toilets, clean, tidy and presentable at all times. I am sure I can cope with this Alfred thought as he went across to the table to have a game of cards before lights out!

After a good night's sleep, again not being in a hurry, Alfred let the other boys go first. Most of them left for work about 07.45 going to the gate straight after the morning count, which was at 07.30. That still left Alfred two hours to get ready for his new job before reporting to the guard on duty at the gate When he got there at the appointed hour Alfred saw three other chaps waiting and they introduced themselves as Otto, Peter and Wolfgang. "My name is Alfred, pleased to meet you;" he replied. They went through the routine of checking out and jumped into the jeep which was waiting for them. The guard who rode with them waited till they had settled in then gave the OK to the driver and off they went. On the way to the Officer's Club Alfred's new companions told him a little about the job. It was not strenuous but you were on the go all the time. The job was two fold. acting as Waiter in the dining room or Steward in any of the three lounges, wearing a white jacket at all times. Between meal duties when doing their other menial tasks they would don a combat jacket. Alfred thanked the boys. "It sounds quite interesting and it will certainly be a new experience waiting on Officers of the American armed forces." Twenty minutes after leaving the Army camp they drove up to an impressive, ornate gate where they were stopped by US guards and had their papers checked before being allowed through to drive up to a large mansion overlooking the Adriatic. The driver took them to the servants' entrance and the guard handed them over to the Sergeant in charge. Inside they were greeted by the morning gang who had already been on the job since 0600. They all had coffee together before laying up the tables in the dining room for lunch and checking that all was in place in the three lounges for serving beverages or alcoholic drinks afterwards.

The more experienced of the two gangs now worked as one taking the orders and serving the meal when ready. Alfred and the 2 other newcomers were told to watch and take notice how the food was served.

Alfred took to this life very quickly, in fact he thought he had never had it so good. Once everybody got used to one another the days ran like clockwork and it was not long before the P.o.Ws. were left to get on with it. In fact the chefs and pastry cooks were looking forward to the boys helping them, never more so than when a national holiday was celebrated. The most celebrated were Independence Day, Thanksgiving, Easter and Christmas. On those days the menu was Roast Turkey and all the trimmings including a cigar for everybody. Preparation began the day before the feast day as soon as the provisions were delivered. Every chef in the Army took pride in serving the perfectly cooked meal on the day. How different in the P.o.W. compound, although the menu was identical and ingredients for the meal the same, as well as a cigar for everyone, the German cooks, their minds geared to German cooking, were unable to make the best of the good food they had before them and in the end requested help from their American counterparts. Not that this worried Alfred and the rest of the gang, as they had their perfectly cooked meal immediately after the last officer had left the dining room. The chef insisted that they sat down and he would serve their meal. Again Alfred thought, "this is living a life of luxury. "Who would have thought he would strike it so lucky, just one thing he missed, his nightly game of cards. In fact the boys working at the club spent very few waking hours back at the main Army camp except on their day off. As it turned out, that was enough for Alfred to land himself in serious trouble.

To make playing cards a little more interesting they used match sticks for stake money. This was satisfactory for a long while but eventually, with everybody now being paid 80 cents a day, money in their pockets amounted to quite a sum. Someone suggested why not use our earnings for stake money. They agreed unanimously to do just that and before long the stakes grew higher and higher. Someone must have informed the Military Authorities about this as one evening in the middle of a game military police raided the camp and found in a number of huts that the boys were playing for money which is strictly forbidden in the American Armed Forces. Those caught playing for money were arrested and removed from the camp for the night. What would happen next and what the punishment might be no one knew but they did not have to wait long to find out.

Next morning they were taken before three American Army officers, acting as trial judges, to be sentenced. The offenders also had an American officer acting as their Defence Counsel. There was little he could do for the boys but plead for leniency as the prisoners were unaware of the rules on gambling. It was the panel of Judges unanimous view that ignorance of the law is no excuse and pronounced sentence for the offenders' heads to be shaven.

At this point Alfred spoke out and reminded the court that this would amount to corporal punishment which was not allowed under the Geneva Convention. The judges made a note and retired to take counsel and after twenty minutes returned to announce final sentence. The senior officer spoke on behalf of the panel of judges saying: "As none of the other offenders objected to the original sentence of having their heads shaved that sentence is final. As for prisoner Zollman, to avoid any lengthy legal case with Geneva we have changed his sentence to be fined a month's wages." Alfred did not know what to say about that and wished now he had kept his mouth shut. After all, hair grows very quickly and would be back where it was now in 6 or 8 weeks time while a month's pay is lost forever. Ah well, Alfred thought, you cannot win them all. It was a gamble which did not come off.

Chapter 23: Where will the journey end?

As the gang who worked at the officer's club got into a rhythm, they found their work very enjoyable and most rewarding. Not only did they improve their skill of how to serve food and drinks correctly, they also learned a lot of new culinary secrets from various chefs, pastry cooks and confectioners under whom they worked, including variations of recipes and a few new ones as well. There were days when there was even enough time to go to the games lounge and play a frame or two of pool as long as it was not occupied by officers.

Time simply flew by and Christmas was almost upon them.All of them thought of their folks at home wondering where they might be and what kind of a Christmas they were facing. The news of the state of war was a gloomy one for the P.o.Ws. The last pockets of resistance by German troops in northern Italy had been dealt with and for the Italians the war was over. In the west the Allied Forces were close to the German border. Whilst in the east the Russians made an all out attempt to be the first in Berlin. There was nothing the boys could do to alleviate the situation back home. Alfred could not help but think, "here am I living a life of luxury. What is the good of bemoaning this fact as it would not help anyone, so I may as well get on and do my work."

As 1945 dawned it became very clear that the war would soon be over. It was just a question of when? As it happened, it was in early May that year, when the German High Command surrendered to the Allies, which saw the victory in Europe, with the bombing stopped and guns fell silent a great sigh of relief went out all over Europe. In the Far East however the war went on unabated. Towards Autumn the first American troops were withdrawn from Italy to return home, or so they hoped. There was always the possibility that some might be shipped to the Far East before they returned to the USA. So it was not long before the first GIs. from the Rimini camp were on the move. Many of the Italians were sorry to see them go, so also was Alfred and the rest of the gang working at the officers' club. With fewer and fewer officers attending, visiting or making use of the facilities which the club offered it became obvious the club would be closed before long. Surprisingly they kept going to see the old year out and the new year in before the place was handed back to the Italian owner.

However, the boys weren't long without a job. Alfred, having basic knowledge of the working and maintenance of petrol and diesel engines, found himself in the motor pool doing just that. Holding a driving licence Alfred was asked to give the vehicles a test run once the servicing was completed, he was thankful for that, being out in the cold and wind made his wound, received a year earlier, very painful. The workshop was not as warm and cosy as the club house, but it was better than working out in the open somewhere. As Spring arrived the Ps.o.W. were told to get their belongings packed as in 2 days time they were to leave what had now become familiar surroundings. On the 7th March 1946 at 0800 they assembled on the parade ground for the last time. The morning count and all other checks completed, the command came; "Right turn, forward march!" With a song on their lips they marched through the gates to the railway station a mile or so away. Again carefully they were counted as they boarded the train. Once all on board the train began to move almost immediately and still nobody had any idea where they were heading.

After a 4 hour ride the train slowed down as they were entering a dock area, but where? Then they spotted a name painted in large letters on a warehouse building, LIVORNO. "Anyone know where that is?" Alfred asked. "Somewhere on the west coast of Italy. Not very far from Pisa." someone piped up. "That is unknown territory to me." Alfred muttered. "We just have to wait and see." What they did see, as they drew alongside the ship, were British Tommies. This was unexpected it must be said, but at least it gave the boys something to think and talk about as well as to speculate where they might be heading. It was from then on that the British took charge of operations. The boys also noticed that British Soldiers were already on board the ship, so surely their destination would be somewhere in Britain. Then the order was given to get off the train but, instead of boarding the ship, the prisoners were led to a holding camp on the dock side and were given a field ration with a hot mug of tea with milk and sugar, a beverage to which the German taste buds were not accustomed. They had better get used to it, as from now on it would be their daily drink.

It was mid-afternoon when they began to board the ship. As they did so, another count was taken to make absolutely sure they would not leave any of their charges behind. Alfred had a quick look round and estimated there were some 500 fellow prisoners on this mystery cruise. On board British soldiers were guiding them to their quarters at the stern of the ship. When those in authority were satisfied all was OK they gave the thumbs up, the gangways were raised, lines were cast off and slowly the ship moved away from the quay, made its way to the port entrance and out into open waters. Going to sea was an entirely new experience for Alfred. He had been up in the air, had thousands of air miles on his record as well as countless parachute jumps, but never, ever had he gone to sea. Here he was embarking on his first sea voyage on an ocean liner. From now on all public announcements were given in English as well as in German and the first of them came as soon as they were on their way. It concerned the emergency drill for all passengers who without exception, had to go to their sleeping quarters, read the emergency instructions then pick up their lifejacket and wait for 5 long blasts from the ship's horn before making their way to their assigned station. That signal was given about 15 minutes later. As everyone had to be accounted for it took quite a while before the count was completed. No search was called for so the ship's company was dismissed and with the time now 18.30 the evening meal was being served and everyone made their way to their allotted restaurant to enjoy the first meal at sea.

Chapter 24: Where will we drop Anchor next?

With the meal over, Alfred and a few others decided, as there was still an hour before curfew, to take the air before getting their bunks ready for the night. On the notice board there was a deck plan indicating the area where the German Ps.o.W. could take their exercise or just take the air between 06.00 and 21.00, which in fact was the same part of the ship where they would assemble in an emergency. Alfred had a quick look at the sky and with the setting sun over the forward bow it told him they were on a westerly course heading for Gibraltar and the Atlantic Ocean.

With a moderate sea throughout the night there was little movement in the ship. Everyone slept well and over breakfast talked and speculated what the daily routine might be. German soldiers were unaccustomed to being transported by sea.

Whilst having their breakfast the Regimental Sergeant Major in charge of the German prisoners came in to tell them: "Look at the notice board. The daily routine for the voyage is pinned there and will not change." This would be: 06.30 reveille followed by breakfast, then morning count and exercises, cleaning

189

the living and sleeping quarters as well as their assigned open deck area. 12.30 lunch and between 14.00 and 16.00 confined to quarters for a rest. Between 16.00 and 18.00 the R.S.M. could be contacted in his cabin. At the same time the ship's doctor was also available if anyone needed him. 18.00 evening count followed by the evening meal. At 20,00 every night there would be a film show in the restaurant showing both American and British movies. 22.00 lights out. However, there was one exception, since none of them had ever been that way before, the day after the next when approaching the Gibraltar Straight, everyone would get the opportunity to have a good look at the Rock of Gibraltar, weather permitting. That would be to starboard, the right side of the ship if you are unfamiliar with shipping terms. To the left, to port, if the weather was right they would see the North African coast and the Atlas Mountains.

First meal of the day over, everybody went on deck for the morning count and then got on with cleaning the part of the ship which they occupied, on deck as well as below deck. For the rest of the day everything went according to plan. Most of the lads went to the movie in the evening. It was a musical in English but that did not matter as there were lots of pretty girls, dancing and romance. Something they had not seen for a long while. All went to bed happily thinking of the girls they left behind, not so Alfred, he preferred a game of cards.

With the sea remaining moderate the night was uneventful. In the morning however, with a good weather forecast, all eagerly looked forward to seeing the Rock, of which everyone had heard but none had seen. As Gibraltar came into view, the sky blue and not a cloud in sight, it was something to behold and to go home and tell the family about. First excitement over, everyone turned to port and were equally impressed seeing the Atlas Mountains in their glory. On they sailed though the Straight and into the Atlantic Ocean where instantly the swell of the sea became more noticeable. That calmed the lads down from the high spirits they had enjoyed at the beginning of the voyage. Towards evening as they neared the notorious Bay of Bisque some of the lads became quite fearful of the rough seas they might encounter but were quickly assured that with clear skies all night a dreaded storm was most unlikely. Just follow the advice given, avoid standing upright, go and lie on your bunk, avoid getting up and in the morning the worst will be over. Most of them had followed the advice and in the morning asked themselves why they had been so worried. Here was a new day and fresh hope that the weather would remain calm.

Alfred did not have such a good and quiet night. During the early morning hours his injured hand began to give him some concern. It began to swell and gave him considerable pain. It also looked red and inflamed by the time they assembled for the morning count. Alfred pointed this out to the sergeant who excused him from work and suggested he lay on his bunk for the rest of the day and then see the doctor at the afternoon surgery. That was exactly what he did and when the doctor saw the hand he was sure that the operation on Alfred's hand was not as successful as first thought by his German counterparts, but somewhat surprised that it took so long to manifest itself. An X-Ray was needed to have a proper diagnosis. All he could do in the meantime was to give him some aspirin to keep the pain down and ice packs to reduce the swelling and inflamation. He would have to go to hospital for the X-Ray and for that a car would be waiting for him at the dock side. Rumour had it that they would be making landfall the day after the next - in about 36 hours time, but where? Alfred did as he was told, took the tablets regularly and renewed the ice pack frequently and was relieved it brought results. He suffered less pain and the swelling went down so that was something to be thankful for. As predicted, 36 hours later they were steaming up Southampton Water to tie up at their allotted berth. After checks and health matters were cleared, Alfred was among the first to go ashore. He had said his goodbyes to the boys he had become friends with, earlier at breakfast time, and after morning count went along the gangway waiting to be called to go through disembarkation. He did not have to wait long and sure enough a car with military escort was waiting for him. It was not a long ride to the hospital but on the way he noticed considerable bomb damage around the dock area. Away from the water front they went through peaceful, tranquil suburban England with folk going about their daily tasks. At the hospital itself he was treated with kindness and professional efficiency. After a period of waiting a doctor, accompanied by an interpreter, showed Alfred the X-Ray and confirmed the ship's doctors diagnosis. The wound had not healed as well as expected and further treatment would be necessary. The hospital would inform the military authorities who would take appropriate action. and then with his guard beside him he was marched through the hospital to the waiting car to take him to a P.o.W camp somewhere in the south of England

Chapter 25: Ganger Camp Romsey

It was some 10minutes later that the car drew into a P.o,W camp. Well Alfred thought, this must be at the edge of Southampton somewhere, 10 minutes is not a very long ride and so it was. It was a transit camp he had been taken to. The reason Alfred understood was, this camp was the nearest to the hospital. The doctors needed to make more tests before they would decide which hospital would be the best to perform the amputation.

Alfred had 4 more visits to the hospital before it was decided a military hospital would be best for the kind of work that needed to be done for this type if injury. Not to idle between hospital visits, Alfred went with one of the working gangs to Southampton docks to help painting the ocean liner, Queen Mary, to get her looking smart for the first crossing to New York with paying passengers since the war.

2 Days after his last visit to the hospital Alfred was told he would be transferred to a larger camp somewhere in Hampshire, so he would be too far away to remain a patient of that hospital. The following morning after breakfast he left the transit camp and within 3 or 4 minutes they were driving through open

and beautiful country. Before long they came to a road junction with a signpost indicating, turn right for Romsey. The driver took that road and after a mile travelling that straight road they entered the country town of Romsey. As they drove through the place Alfred had the impression, to live there, would be quiet and peaceful. At another junction they turned into a road indicating they were on the way to Winchester.

As they left the little market town of Romsey behind them the road went through lovely wooded countryside and it was not long after that they turned into an equally beautiful country lane. Half a mile down that lane the driver stopped outside large gates and told the guard at the gate he had a P.o.W. on board. "Yes" the guard said, "we were expecting him." He opened the gate, waved them on and through they went coming to a final halt outside the office block. The guard who had accompanied Alfred from the camp in Southampton took him into the clerk's office for a routine identity check, then he returned to his unit in Southampton.

Alfred was called before the Sergeant, from a German Infantry Regiment, responsible for the discipline of prisoners in Ganger Camp and was introduced to the daily routine and week-end timetable. All very simple and uncomplicated. Alfred's fellow prisoners welcomed him warmly as it was a happy camp and they had a good relationship with the military authorities. The Sergeant called his clerk in and asked him to take Alfred to hut 9 where there were two vacancies. "Just drop your luggage and the go to the dining hut and have a bite to eat before you do anything else." the sergeant called after Alfred. "Thank you, Sergeant, I will." replied Alfred as he made his way to hut 9. He found the accommodation clean and tidy and chose the empty bed just inside the door as he did not fancy walking the length of the hut every time he came in or went out. It was not difficult finding the dining hut as it was well signposted. The boys expected him and had a plate of cold meats with some slices of bread and a mug of tea ready waiting for him. Whilst Alfred was enjoying his lunch the lads in the kitchen, naturally enough, wanted to know where he came from, where he has been and what was wrong with his hand. Alfred told them enough about himself as he felt they needed to know. Back in the hut he lay on his bed stretched himself out and went to sleep at once.

At 16.30 the first gangs returned from working locally in or around Romsey. One and all were surprised to find a newcomer in the camp. They introduced themselves to Alfred one by one and this went on until meal time when they all went to the dining hut together. One of the last gang to get back was a group of 6 working on a large farm near Winchester. Two of them were from hut 9 of which one was a 20 year old with very blond hair who was a Berliner. Everybody called him Blondie. One did not need three guesses to tell where he came from as he spoke with a distinct Berliner accent. Blondie happened to sit next to Alfred during the evening meal and they struck up a conversation. As Alfred came from Silesia they had something in common. Blondie's father was born in that province and his mother's family had their roots in that part of Germany as well. That's how their friendship began. All this happened during the summer months of 1946. It was during that time Blondie had a letter from his sister Ella. In addition to the family news and whereabouts of their siblings, she wondered if there was some lonely soul in in the camp she could write to as a pen friend. Blondie mentioned this to Alfred who was delighted to take up this offer and began to write to her within days and that relationship blossomed as time went by.

A week after Alfred's arrival at Ganger Camp during breakfast an orderly from the office came to tell Alfred that the doctor wanted to see him at the surgery before he began his work. Visiting hours by the doctor were 09.00-10.00. Anyone not gone out to work could then consult the doctor about their ailments. Alfred had a good idea what this was all about, although the pain in his injured hand and the swelling were under control but showing no sign of healing any further. Just after 9 o'clock he made his way across to the surgery and joined the queue. He did not have to wait too long, and when in the consulting room the doctor told him that on Monday morning he would be taken to a military hospital where, on Tuesday all being well, the little finger on his left hand would be amputated. He would spend another night in hospital and if things went as planned, would be back in camp for supper on Wednesday evening. He would see Alfred the following morning. "My word," Alfred thought, that was quick. In the evening Alfred told his friends about it, who were all pleased that something was to be done about it so quickly.

The weekend ran its usual course with cleaning the huts and public buildings and attending to personal laundry thus keeping the camp neat and tidy. In the afternoon, weather permitting, most chaps went to see the football match taking place in the meadow adjoining the camp, loaned by the farmer who owned the land. Some of the guards also went along. It was a round-robin competition, hut playing hut. Every now and then a camp eleven played a team of British soldiers, on those occasions even most of the officers made an appearance.

Those not interested in football took a stroll into town and watched how the locals spent their Saturday afternoon. Some of the more enterprising boys of the camp found a little job in pubs and hotel bars washing glasses and cleaning the premises, as labour was in rather short supply. In return they had a pint of beer on the quiet, and a sandwich. The beer was a local brew. Strong's of Romsey. On Sunday mornings, with no work to be done Alfred, like many of the boys, wrote home to their family or a girlfriend back home waiting for them to return. Unlike the others Alfred never knew whether or not his letters would ever reach his parents. Officially they were displaced persons and so far had not found a permanent address, but he lived in hope.

As usual on Sundays the canteen opened at 10.00, The barbers were waiting, the post office was open and the general store ready for business. Alfred and Blondie always went together to see if there was any mail for them. Blondie's sister Ella, in Berlin, had written to him asking if there was anyone who would like to receive a letter from home and he had suggested Alfred so a correspondence began between them. Since then Alfred had at least one letter waiting for him every Sunday, sometimes even two. Blondie ceased to hear from the family direct, any news came via Alfred so he had to be content to hear from any of his cousins every now and then.

As for Sunday afternoon, weather permitting, many of the lads went for a walk ending up in Romsey, usually at the Baptist church who served them an afternoon tea. After that they joined the congregation for evening worship and then made their way back to camp. The Sunday afternoon before Alfred had his operation he joined none of these activities. He knew from experience it is best to rest and keep blood pressure down and the heart beating steady. What lay ahead of him he had no idea.

Chapter 26: A new conception of British philosophy

An early start for Alfred on Monday morning. He had to report at the guardhouse at 06.30 to catch the06.58 train for Southampton but had arranged with the kitchen to have a packed lunch to eat on the journey but he had a cup of tea before leaving camp. When he reported at the guard house his escort was waiting for him. Alfred popped into the car and off they went making for Romsey railway station. They did not have to wait long before the train for Southampton arrived.

On arrival at Southampton they changed for the fast train to London. Once they were on their way Alfred began to tuck into his sandwiches. As was his nature he invited his escort to share them, and surprisingly the escort accepted. In return the escort offered Alfred to share the drink from his flask. As they journeyed on the escort explained things of interest. He gave quite a detailed account about Winchester, the former Capital of England, Basingstoke a sleepy little market town and on to Wokingham where they left the train. Again transport was waiting. The ride to the hospital took about 20 minutes where they drew up outside the military wing. Alfred's escort took him to the reception desk where the Matron was waiting for him. She was there to welcome him not knowing how good his command of English was. She herself spoke perfect German which impressed Alfred. Matron helped Alfred with the registration and when completed dismissed the escort and took Alfred to his room. She told him to change into his hospital clothes as before long a nurse would come and take his blood pressure and his pulse. The nurse would also give him some pills and instruction when to take them. A number of tests would be carried out before he had one more X-Ray. Should he have any problems he was to tell someone to let Matron know about his concern. On that note she left to let him get on with it. Alfred was pleased about the X-Ray as his hand as well as being swollen also pained him quite a lot.

Sure enough soon afterwards a nurse arrived and explained very slowly, in English, what she would be doing. She was pleased with the results of the two tests and Alfred thought by taking it easy and resting the previous day he had been very sensible. Tests completed the nurse took him to the X-Ray department and handed him over to the staff there. Alfred had already had a number of X-Rays taken on his previous visit to hospital in Italy so he knew what was coming. The Radiologist took three images of his hand to make quite sure the doctor had a perfect picture of the part of the hand that needed to be operated on. A member of the department then took him to a treatment room where the final tests would take place. Those completed Alfred was taken back to his room and was pleased to lie on his bed and relax as the morning had taken more out of him than he thought it would. Just before lunch the matron looked in inquiring how he felt. She also told Alfred what would happen in the afternoon. "Some time this afternoon a team of doctors, including the surgeon, will call on you to explain tomorrow's procedure. I will be with them and if there is anything you want to know ask them. Now enjoy your lunch and have a rest." With that she left.

It was quite a while since Alfred had enjoyed a meal so much as it had been some 6 hours since he had had his last bite, being the sandwiches he shared with his escort on the train. No wonder he felt peckish and it might well be 24 hours or more before he would have his next substantial meal. Meal over he stretched himself out on his bed and within minutes was sound asleep. About half past two an attendant woke him with a cup of tea suggesting Alfred get ready as before long the surgeon would be along to talk to him.

It was just after three in the afternoon when the Matron and three doctors arrived. Alfred stood up as the party entered his room., one female and two male doctors. The lady doctor came across to him shook his hand introducing herself as Philippa Broadstone, Surgeon Lieutenant Commander and explained that she would be the person performing the operation and the other two doctors would assist her. These were Dr. Pern and Dr. Edelman who would assist with the procedure. The Surgeon spoke to Alfred in German all the time and mentioned that if her German was not good enough she could always consult Matron who spoke perfect German. "There will be no need for that," Alfred assured the lady surgeon; "You speak very good German." She told him he would be the first on the list the following morning. If all goes well, and I do not see why it should not, you will be back in your room before lunch. We will keep you here overnight and you should be back in Romsey late on Wednesday afternoon. "The three of us will do our best, so don't worry. See you in the morning." With that they all left.

When he was alone Alfred looked at his hand which was now very swollen. Not only that, he also had acute pain. The usual painkillers had little effect now and he was glad something was to be done about it in the morning but this was still hours away. As there was still some time before the evening meal and bed time he looked through the Picture Post magazine and others like it. Most of them were full of pictures and stories of the preparations that were being made by Buckingham Palace, as well as the Government, for the forthcoming marriage between Princess Elizabeth and Prince Philip of Greece and Denmark in November 1947. Looking through these magazines made him feel rather drowsy and he fell asleep, understandably as after all, it had been a long and tiring day and sleep could do him nothing but good. Alfred was served only a light meal in the evening which suited him fine, and after the nurse had given him his medicine he went straight to bed and had a good night.

Another early awakening for Alfred on Tuesday. This time it was a nurse who roused him from sleep offering him a glass of water. Any other beverage or food had to wait until after the operation. The previous day Dr. Edelman had indicated that a nurse would begin preliminary preparation before he left his room for the Operating Theatre so as to be ready to begin the procedure at the scheduled time of 09.00. Alfred was now pretty drowsy when porters came to wheel him to the theatre. In fact the next thing he could remember was waking up in the recovery room. Once he stirred, the nurse went to tell doctor Pern who appeared a few minutes later. He checked Alfred's heart beat, blood pressure and lungs and assured Alfred all was well.

Matron also was informed and looked in on Alfred to see how he felt before he was taken back to his room. She told him that surgeon Broadstone would come to see him later that afternoon.

Back in his room Alfred enjoyed the hot cup of sweet tea offered to him and then lay on his bed to assess the situation. Looking at his bandaged left hand, now short of the damaged finger, he felt a strange sensation where it had once been. He could hardly describe it and the hand felt slightly unbalanced. At the same time next to the ring finger he sensed an itch, yet there was no finger to scratch, all very strange. This is something I will have to get used to he told himself. Then he relaxed, dropped off to sleep and woke up when lunch was being served, again this was a very light meal after this Alfred felt much better. Satisfied with the whole outcome he stretched out on his bed and slept some more. In fact it was Matron who woke him telling him that the Surgeon was on her way. When Dr. Broadstone came into the room she exclaimed; "My word you are looking well, keep it up. The amputation went according to the book and the wound should heal well. I cannot see any complication arising. Your temperature and blood pressure are normal. Heart beat is strong, lungs sound, kidneys are working. If we find you in the same state of health in the morning, and I can't see why not, then you can go back to Romsey. I shall be looking in on you just after 08.00 to see how you are. Matron will see to it that all travelling papers are ready for your return to camp. Till tomorrow then." She shook hands with Alfred and went to see her next patient. Matron too was pleased all went well and wished Alfred a quick recovery.

After everybody had gone Alfred sat back in his chair and thought to himself that this must all be a dream. Here I am in hospital in a country with which Germany was at war just over a year ago. You could still see the evidence of devastation caused by German air raids. The hearts of the people were still aching and grieving over the loss and suffering of human lives. One could see some of it in this very hospital he was in now. Yet he had received nothing but kindness and was treated with professional courtesy by all who were involved in treating his wound received in the bloody battle at Monte Casino. This was just the opposite from the picture and images painted by German Nazi propaganda. What a lucky chap he was to end up in Britain. He had to admit, that forming the British character and British values, the Christian faith must have had a lot to do with it. Still feeling the effects of the anaesthetic in him he dropped off to sleep again and this drowsiness remained with him for the rest of the day. "Best not to struggle against it," Alfred thought, "just let the day run its course," which it did, with nurses coming and going checking temperature and blood pressure, administering pills of one kind and another with kitchen staff serving food and drink, Alfred knew it, it was lights out.

Wednesday morning brought another early morning call. The nurse had quite a job to wake Alfred out of his deep sleep and reminded him that the surgeon would be calling on him to check whether or not he was fit to return to camp. The surgeon called just after eight o'clock and asked Alfred how he felt, had the pain eased. She saw the swelling had gone down and enquired how his appetite was, to which Alfred could only answer that it was good. Satisfied with the answers the surgeon inspected the hand which was already showing signs of healing. "Barring any infection in the immediate future you should be alright. Make sure you have the stitches removed in a week's time. Good luck in the future and I am pleased I could be of help." Shaking hands with Alfred she handed him over to Matron and left. Matron too was pleased all had gone well and that she had been of some service to him. "When you are ready come and see me in my office and I will give you your papers and some instructions for the camp doctor. Your escort will be waiting."

As far as Alfred was concerned there was not much, apart from a few items of toiletries, to get ready. At Matron's office his escort was waiting so were his papers as well as a packed lunch for two. Now that was very noble thought Alfred, and he said so to Matron. He thanked her in his limited American English which he had picked up in Italy, and asked for his heartfelt thanks to be passed on to all the staff who had looked after him whilst in their care. He and his escort then left Matron's office and got into the Jeep which would take them to Wokingham.

Chapter 27: Experiencing British Life and Culture

The return journey to Romsey was uneventful, as expected About noon Alfred and his escort opened the parcel of sandwiches the chef in the hospital had prepared for them. The camp had been informed of Alfred's return on Wednesday but not knowing which train they might catch could not arrange for a car to meet them. "Well," the escort said to Alfred, "We have no choice but to walk back to the camp." "That's alright with me," answered Alfred. "We can take the back road which runs almost parallel with the main road to Winchester It will save us nearly a mile by not going first into the town centre." "You know the way?" the escort asked. "Sure do." replied Alfred, and off they went.

Half an hour later they came to the lane which passed the camp, and there just a hundred yards or so to the left they saw the entrance. The escort must have felt relieved seeing the camp even though he did not say so. At the gate the guard checked the papers and let them through. Alfred and escort went straight to the office to report his return. The escort handed over the relevant papers then went out to a waiting car which would take him back to his Unit in Winchester. Alfred was told that the doctor would see him on Friday morning and that he was excused from doing any work for the rest of the week. "Glad to see you back Zollman," said the clerk as Alfred was leaving the office. "Happy to be back." answered Alfred and made his way to Hut 9.

Nothing in the Hut had changed of course, so as he was exhausted from his tiring day, he went to his bed and lay on it to rest for a while. It would not be long now before the first of the boys returned from work. Most days it was the Gang who worked on the Broadlands Estate who were back first and today was no exception. Everybody was pleased to see him "home" again so to speak, as they told him that life in the evenings was pretty dull without him "Well I never," thought Alfred, "I had not realised I was so popular." One by one the boys returned and all wanted to know how he had got on. "Well, I had a great surprise. I never thought that a woman, a Lady Surgeon, would perform the operation." Alfred told them. "Was she beautiful?" the boys wanted to know "She was absolutely charming, kind and considerate." By the time Alfred had said hello to everybody it was time to get ready for the evening meal. When Blondie was ready they both made their way across to the dining hut and caught up on any news and gossip from in and around the camp. Meal over and back in their hut Alfred felt he had had enough excitement for the day so lay on his bed and was soon fast asleep.

Next morning he reported to the doctor who removed the bandage from the injured hand and was very pleased with what he saw, the wound looked healthy and was already showing signs of healing. The doctor gave him some pain relief tablets should he need them. Being excused from doing any work the lads, as before, left him to sweep and tidy up their quarters for the daily inspection later in the morning. Then he rested for the remainder of the day and it paid off. He began to feel more like himself again, certainly well enough to have a game of cards, and that was saying something. So the weeks passed and it was September before Alfred joined a gang working on the Broadlands Estate. With excessive rain throughout the summer some of the grain harvest had yet to be gathered and the potatoes had to be lifted and stored as well as the other root crops. The help of the P.o.W. was still vital and very much appreciated by the farming community. They showed it by always treating them courteously. Often the farmers brought them a drop of milk and sugar for their tea or some cigarettes. On arrival they were always greeted with a smile and at the end of the day's work left them with a "Thank You!"

Early in October the British government eased restrictions on the distance P.o.W.s could go. Unaccompanied the distance remained at 7 miles but if accompanied by a British citizen they could go beyond the 7-mile limit provided the camp authorities were informed and they were back in camp by 22.00. It was part of government policy to engender greater fraternity with German prisoners. The hope was that some British families would invite prisoners to spend part of Christmas with them. Many farmers who had men from Ganger Camp working for them throughout the summer and autumn and farmed within an hours drive of the camp invited the boys for Christmas dinner not just out of human kindness but also to say thank you for helping to gather in the harvest in what was, weather wise, a very difficult year. Alfred and Blondie drew the short straw here as the Broadlands Estate had too many men working for it to entertain such an idea. The farm Blondie worked on was too far away to make it possible for the farmer, a Mr. Straton, to make the round trip within the time. The two of them, with the rest of the boys left in the camp, had their Christmas dinner and afterwards strolled into town and went to Evensong in the Abbey at 15.30 where they were

213

warmly welcomed. After the service they went to the town centre to see what was going on but found it absolutely deserted. This did not surprise them at all. They took the short cut back to camp. As they made their way back through the housing estate one of the residents called after them to come and have some Christmas cake and a cup of tea, an offer the two of them could not refuse. As Alfred looked back on the day, his first Christmas in Britain, he could not but help comparing with the previous year's Christmas in Italy with the Americans. There they had plenty to eat but lacked the human touch and personal kindness that forms human relationships which they had found in Britain

After the harvest had been gathered in, seasonal workers on the land were no longer required so with the Christmas holidays over and the New Year welcomed, everybody was assigned to new jobs of which most of them were taken up in the supply industry. Although many Soldiers, Naval Personal and Airmen were demobilised there still existed a shortage of labour. With hundreds of P.O.W. at the disposal of the government, the minister in charge of supplies made the most of this labour force to keep supply lines open. So it happened that Alfred and 29 of his camp mates were assigned to a vast supply depot about 10 miles from Romsey. It was huge with large stores but it lacked loading bays which, Alfred thought, would make loading and unloading child's play Lorries were coming and going all day long and the whole gang was delighted to have landed such a good placement. With the temperature falling almost every day this meant that for at least half the time they would be inside the sheds out of the biting wind. It was a busy place, but how long would this good fortune last?

Alfred need not to have worried as a week or so after the gang from Ganger Camp had begun working at the depot, quite by chance the manager discovered that not only could Alfred ride a motor bike but also drive cars, vans and trucks. Naturally enough the manager, a Mr. White, asked Alfred how such a young man had gained all this knowledge and the skills of motor transport as well as the combustion engine so Alfred told him as best he could of his military training. The manager was delighted to hear this. You are just the kind of chap I need on the place. You can be our despatch rider and use any vehicle needed to take goods and parcels from one end of the depot to the other. I will do my best to keep you here as long as you are at Ganger Camp," and so it turned out.

Not only did the temperatures drop in January 1947, but they also had heavy snow falls at the end of the month with more to come in February. Temperatures too never rose above freezing day or night, the kind of winter no one wanted. The government certainly did not, nor did industry or the farming fraternity, or the good citizens of Britain. They had suffered enough in recent years. The boys in camp too wondered how to keep warm. Every Saturday afternoon they roamed through the woods and coppices, of which there were quite a number near the camp, gathering wood to supplement their coal ration and keep the home fires burning. As none of the farmers complained or laid a charge against the P.o.W. the Commanding Officer of the camp saw no reason to take any action. After all the prisoners were in his care and he was responsible for their well-being. Whatever the weather life went on except for one day towards the end of February. As Blondie returned to camp in the evening he was called to the office where he was told that in the morning he would start on a new assignment with a small team of two. Eric Vandervelt in hut 4 would be his partner and it would be on a small-holding with 5 acres of orchard. They had to be ready to leave after the morning count. When Blondie returned to hut 9, Alfred asked him what they had wanted him for so he told all of them about his new placement in Botley.

March came with no sign of any change in the weather. In fact there was more snow forecast and later in the month freezing rain with winds continuing from the east. However, towards the end of March the weather did begin to change and although night frosts continued, at least day temperatures began to recover and rose steadily. Even so work on the farms was almost at a standstill as the ground was still frozen.

The supply industry had their own problems during this cold winter. With everything still in short supply only the main roads and bus routes were treated to keep the traffic and supplies going and the speed limit was reduced in the hope of reducing accidents. All this interrupted the smooth flow at the supply depot and the boys from the camp could do little about it. All they could do was to keep the lorries on the move. Eventually the weather changed, the sun came out and the frost went. Everywhere now it was full steam ahead especially on the land. Then one day early in May when returning from work Blondie said to Alfred: "What do you think, the family asked if I would like to be billeted with them." "Gracious me," is all Alfred could think of to say; "How do you feel about it?" Blondie's reply was "I would like to go. They are nice people, kind and caring. They make me feel like one of the family." "If you feel like that," Alfred said, "then you should go. I'll miss you dear friend and wish you the best of luck." That was the last thing Alfred had expected to hear and it proves how unexpected life can be. The day before Blondie left the camp he gave an invitation to Alfred from the family, inviting him to have lunch and tea with them on the last Sunday in June when Blondie came for his monthly visit. Now who could resist an invitation like that and Alfred accepted straight away.

Chapter 28: British home life

That Sunday in June could not come too soon for Alfred. He was really looking forward to this and Meeting the family on the appointed Sunday. Blondie and Gladys, the daughter of the family, arrived in her car just on 10.00. Blondie came into the camp, collected his mail and bought just one or two items in the shop which the family had not so far provided. Business completed Alfred and Blondie walked to the car where Blondie introduced Gladys to Alfred and visa versa.

On the way to Botley Alfred and Blondie caught up on family and camp news and gossip whilst at the same time Alfred enjoyed the ride through the countryside. On arrival at Gladys' home in Botley she introduced Alfred to her parents, Bill and Polly Gannaway. While she helped her mother with the lunch Blondie showed Alfred his bedroom which was almost a bed-sitter. Alfred was most impressed by it all as he was with the roast lunch. "Now that is what you might call home cooking!" said Alfred, pointing to the food on the table. He certainly enjoyed every mouthful as he did his dessert, a large portion of apple tart, one of Gladys' mother's specialities. Who can blame Blondie taking up the invitation to be billeted there. After lunch they all enjoyed a rest, deservedly so for Polly, who had worked hard all morning to produce such a wonderful meal. Later on the boys helped with the washing up and then before tea fed, watered and bedded down the live-stock.

All too soon it was time for Alfred to return to camp. As they left, Polly extended another invitation in two months time. "I am looking forward to that. Thank you very much." said Alfred and in continental style kissed Polly's hand as he said good bye. During the journey back to camp in Gladys' car for some strange reason his mind went back to Crete. He thought of the Marine, about his age, who guarded him for a few days and then became his prisoner. Did he get through the war unscathed Alfred wondered, if so, where would he be now? That young Marine Alfred was thinking of, Vincent by name, never lived more than 25 miles away from Romsey for the rest of his life.

Alfred was very much looking forward to his next visit to Botley in two months time and the weeks went by in a flash. The atmosphere at Gladys' home when he returned was quiet and peaceful as well as relaxing. Gladys' family made both Blondie and Alfred feel like one of them. Throughout the meal Alfred felt that Blondie appeared fidgety and he began to wonder what it might be. As they were helping with the washing up Blondie confided in him that he and Gladys had become engaged to be married. This was not at all what Alfred expected to hear.

"Well, congratulations to you both. When is the big day going to be?" "Early in the New Year if all goes well. I have told the family back home about it but so far had no reply. It will be interesting to hear what my dear sister has to say when next she writes to you" replied Blondie. "Good luck to you. I'll let you know what she thinks. The boys in the camp will be pleased to hear the news that I do know" said Alfred. As always the time passed all too quickly and as Alfred was leaving with Blondie and Gladys in the car for the journey back to Romsey, Polly mentioned the 72 hours Christmas leave which the government granted to prisoners if they had someone to stand surety for them. "Would you like to spend Christmas with us?" Polly asked. "Would I!" said Alfred. "Thank you very much. I'll be looking forward to it."

Alfred now had two items of news to tell the boys back in the camp. Lucky me and lucky Blondie he thought. Christmas was three months away and in the meantime there was his job at the Supply Depot where he had a kind of promotion. The manager now let him decide the order of priority for the goods to be despatched and to make sure the good relationship between the management and the gang from the camp continued. Alfred also heard from Ella in Berlin saying that all the family were pleased Blondie had found happiness in England and he told Blondie so when he next came to collect his mail.

There were other exciting events happening in the country at the time. In November of 1947.the heiress to the British Throne, HRH Princess Elizabeth, married Prince Philip of Greece who had been serving in the RN during the war. When it became public that the couple would spend the first part of their honeymoon on the Broadlands Estate, the whole of Romsey became excited, including the occupants of Ganger Camp. Their planned arrival on the day was for late afternoon or early evening and that fitted in well with the routine of the camp. Immediately after the evening meal on the day of the royal couple's wedding, most of the boys made their way the quarter of a mile to the main road leading from Winchester to Romsey and lined the street mixing with the local population cheering the newly-weds as they passed by. November over, Alfred could hardly wait for Christmas to come as that would mean two nights sleeping in a feather bed plus a warm house and an open log fire.

Chapter 29: Christmas in an English Home

On Christmas Eve at 14.00, Gladys and Blondie came to the camp to take Alfred back home with them for the Christmas holidays. The route to Botley had now become quite a familiar one. Polly was waiting for them with a cup of tea and after Alfred had taken his few belongings into the bedroom the two youngsters went out to feed the stock and shut them up for the night. That finished the work for the day and the rest of the evening was theirs. After the evening meal they played cards and for a change one or two board games. The card games were unfamiliar to Alfred, but being Alfred he learned fast. As for the board games, they were easy enough to follow. Gladys reminded them that they had to rise early to be in church the next day by 07.00. Earlier in the evening they had all discussed about going to church and both Alfred and Blondie said they were happy to accompany her for the early service. As the boys were ready to get into bed they experienced some difficulties getting between the sheets and on investigating what the trouble might be they discovered the ladies of the house had had some fun with them by making apple-pie beds! They also concealed between sheets and blankets brushes and other small items which needed to be traced and removed before they were able to get some sleep. All this was intended and it caused some amusement and laughter for the ladies who stood in the hall by the bedroom door.

On Christmas Day Gladys made sure the lads were up and ready for church. She need not have worried as both of them were used to rising early. They made it to church in good time where they were warmly welcomed by the Verger who went straight to the Vestry to tell the Rector about their visitors. The congregation at this early service were mostly farmers and growers and people working with live-stock. With no midnight service in those days the numbers attending were large. As Blondie had already been attending services at the church he did not find it difficult to follow. However, Alfred having been brought up in the Roman Catholic tradition could also follow the service without difficulty. At the end of the service the Rector closed with a prayer spoken in German and that gesture made the boys' Christmas very special.

The first job after returning home was attending to the live stock, which the boys saw to, while the ladies prepared breakfast. When everybody had finished breakfast the ladies started preparing the Christmas dinner while the boys went and collected eggs in the hen houses. Bill, with no papers to read, felt a little lost, so he made it his business to bring in enough firewood for the open fire into the living room to make sure family and visitor enjoyed a cosy evening.

When it was time to serve Christmas dinner, most of it home produced, Alfred really was looking forward to comparing the difference between the German, American and British way. There was no doubt in his mind it was thumbs up for the British way. Here Alfred experienced home cooking at its best. Polly served a truly scrumptious meal. From the beginning to the end, the first course to the last. Immediately the meal was over and dishes cleared off the table it was time to open the Christmas presents. Neither Alfred nor Blondie had ever taken part in this British tradition as in Germany presents were exchanged on Christmas Eve. There were three parcels for the boys. The one for Alfred, a present to him from the Gannaway family, contained a shirt for which the coupons were donated by Bill. Blondie too found a shirt in his parcel, this time the coupons were sacrificed by Gladys. This all came as a great surprise to the boys. They in turn were only able to give small tokens in return. Still being P.o.W. the money they did have could only be spent in the camp canteen. Alfred gave Gladys a box of note paper and

Blondie bought a fountain pen for her. The boys had been concerned as to what to give to Polly and Bill but thanks to Gladys they need not have worried' For mother there was a bouquet of flowers and for father an ounce of his favourite tobacco, for which Gladys had given them the money. For that it must be said the two boys were very thankful.

Now it was time to get on with the work. Alfred and Blondie saw to the washing up, and there was plenty of that, whilst Gladys and her father went to see to the animals and mother took a well deserved rest. All finished just in time to gather round the wireless to listen to the King's Christmas message to country and the Commonwealth. For the rest of the afternoon they continued to listen to the wireless broadcasting light music and entertainment, the family trying the best they could to explain what was going on. After the evening meal it was back to card and board games until bedtime. With this ended a wonderful Christmas Day thanks to the kindness and generosity of the Gannaway family.

Boxing Day, and return to camp, came all too soon for Alfred. Still, there was breakfast as first thing then the animals needed attention and there was lunch to be had before Alfred needed to pack his few belongings before saying: "Thank you and Aufwiedersehen;" to this lovely family. On the way back Blondie asked Alfred to be Best Man at his wedding. Alfred readily agreed and was looking forward to it, providing there were no objections from the British Authorities.

Chapter 30: Life in London

Come January 2nd everybody went back to work. Many of the boys were very happy to do so as life in the camp was on the brink of becoming boring. The British authorities did their best to provide some entertainment over the holidays. The films shown in the camp were all in English of course and many of the lads found them difficult to understand. Not that this bothered Alfred he was quite happy and content to play cards every evening with those who were like minded.

Then four days into the New Year on his return from work Alfred was told to report to the office. When he got there the Sergeant said he had good news for him. In the morning post there were his discharge documents. As the only professional Soldier in the camp and one with the longest serving record he was among the first to be repatriated. Alfred was dumb struck, he just did not know what to say because that was the last thing he expected. Once the news sank in however, he was very pleased to hear it. The Sergeant also told him that the British government offered a contract to all P.o.W. for repatriation to remain in Britain to work on either the land, in mines or on a short contract. This was helping at the venues required for the Olympic Games to be held in London later in the summer. That last offer was for 4 months and would end on the 31st May. Accommodation and 3 meals a day would be provided and a pair of overalls. In addition he would be paid £2.00 Sterling a week for spending money. "Go away and think about it Zollman;" said the Sergeant; "and let me know within 48 hours of your decision." With that Alfred left the office and back in the hut everybody wanted to know what the Sergeant wanted him for. Alfred told them that he would leave the camp at the end of January and about the contracts the British government were offering those who were to be repatriated.

The offer to work in London and earn some money was very tempting. With careful spending he might even have some money to take home with and not arrive penniless. So he decided to stay and told the Sergeant so the following day. Alfred also requested that a letter to Blondie in Botley might be posted telling him the news and his regret at not being able to be his Best Man at his forthcoming wedding to Gladys in February.

Needless to say Blondie was bitterly disappointed Alfred could not be at his wedding but in reply wished him all the best for the future. Blondie was not the only one to be disappointed about Alfred leaving Ganger

Camp, so was the manager of the supply depot who considered him to be a great loss to the workforce.

The next three weeks simply flew by. There were a number of forms to be filled in and the contract to work in London to be completed and signed. The final few days in Ganger Camp were just routine. Out to work in the morning and playing cards in the evening. Alfred made the most of playing cards, for heaven only knew when next he would have the opportunity to do so.

On the 31st January he said good bye to the lads in the hut one by one as they left for work and just after 09.00 went through the camp gates for the last time to be taken by car to Romsey station to catch the train for London as hehad done before going to hospital to have his finger amputated. Again he changed trains at Southampton. This time it was to the end of the line, Waterloo Station, London.

As Alfred went through the platform gates on to the forecourt looking for signs and direction notices he spotted the station clock. The time was 12.06 and right underneath a sign in English and German and an arrow indicating the gathering point for foreign workers only a few yards away. Alfred made his way there, went in to the room to the reception desk and presented his papers which were thoroughly checked and then handed back to him. Looking around the room whilst the desk clerk read through them he noticed further back in the room an area laid out as a small café with young men enjoying a bowl of soup and a roll as well as a cup of tea. What struck Alfred most, when casting his eyes around was, that there was not one military uniform in sight. The staff that dealt with the paper work were all male, smartly dressed and all spoke German.

After receiving his papers back the man who seemed to be in charge came over to Alfred and invited him to collect his bowl of soup, roll and cup of tea and find himself a seat. As he made his way to the counter he heard two chaps speaking in German on the other side of the room. With his tray of goodies in his hands he went across to them and introduced himself. "Alfred is my name." They introduced themselves as Sven and Walter. Alfred very quickly learned that these lads stayed behind in Britain to earn a little money before returning home. Not everyone gathered in the room were German Alfred discovered later. Some came from Italy, others from the Balkan countries. About three o'clock in the afternoon those assembled in the room were told to gather their belongings and make their way to the bus waiting on the road to take them to the Olympic Village. On the way through London scars of the war were still very much in evidence and it was quite a while before they arrived at their destination. They were taken to the part of the Olympic village that was completed and in use. It was a good opportunity for the organisers of the games to test the living quarters for the athletes to see everything was working alright including facilities such as lighting, security, plumbing and catering. As they entered the building with the living quarters they were assigned a room furnished for two with two single beds, a washbasin and a wardrobe. Toilets were along the corridor. Alfred's room mate for the next three months was to be a chap by the name of Max from Hannover. Max was a couple of years younger than Alfred and had served in one of the tank regiments and was taken prisoner in Normandy. They freshened up and went together to the dining hall for their evening meal which was at 18.30. During the meal they learned about their assignment. Alfred was to work at the sports hall, a vast, covered arena where the gymnastics were to be held as well as indoor ball games. The outer walls were already up and the roof was on. Work to fit out the interior was scheduled to begin the next day. "That suits me fine," Alfred thought. My time as a Paratrooper taught me a lot about building and erecting defences that would last." His room mate Max was to be employed as a labourer where ever help was needed. Working hours were from 08.00 - 17.00 with an hour lunch break. Double deck buses to take them to their place of work would leave from outside their accommodation at 07.30. They were to make sure they were on them. Breakfast would be served from 06.00. As Alfred had a long day travelling and facing new challenges as well as new faces around him he began to feel tired and opted for an early night.

After a good night's sleep Alfred felt rested and was eagerly looking forward to this new adventure helping to build something that would last. What's more, he would have a hand in staging the 1948 Olympics Games in London. He got on well with the other workers and most were British. Alfred soon picked up was needed and how the foreman wanted it done. After a week in this new environment he was looking forward to next week and hoped he could see the whole project through to its completion. As time went by and the project was taking shape, leading figures in politics paid a visit to the site. Among them was the Prime Minister Clement Attlee, the leader of the Opposition Winston Churchill and from the Royal Family HRH the Princess Margaret. Every time one of these VIPs came to visit, worked stopped on the site they were visiting for twenty minutes to half an hour whilst the visitors looked at the work that had so far been completed and spoke to some of the workers. When they were leaving they were sent on their way with loud cheers and applause. These occasions were the highlight of the day as far as Alfred was concerned.

All too soon the end of May arrived and it was time to say good bye not only to the people he worked with but also to the project he had been working on for the last four months. Apart from some cosmetic work the stadium was ready for use. On the 21st of May Alfred gathered his few belongings, wished his roommate Max all the best for the future and went to the office to collect his pay, some £12 in one pound notes, and his travel vouchers. He then caught the bus that would take him to Liverpool Street Station to board a train for Harwich from where a ferry would sail to the Hook of Holland on the continent. Before Alfred went on to the platform to take his seat on the train he went to change his £12 Sterling to West German currency. He knew the restrictions on the amount of Pound Sterling one could take abroad were strictly enforced. He was looking for a trouble free sailing, no hiccups. On the dot of time the train moved slowly on its way gathering speed as it left the urban part of London behind. It arrived at the docks at Harwich on time, coming to a halt alongside the ferry which was due to sail at 13.00

for her seven hour journey to Hook of Holland. Alfred thought, given fair weather and a favourable wind there might still be an hour of daylight when they reached their destination. That would be helpful to the passengers as they made their way across to the trains that would take them to their destinations. His was the overnight train to Berlin.

Chapter 31: Berlin here we come!

As it turned out, Alfred's predictions were right. The sea was calm, the wind light and from the north and the ferry docked at The Hook well ahead of schedule. The trains were ready and waiting to take the passengers to their various destination in Europe. Before Alfred boarded the train for Berlin he stopped at the snack stall to buy something to eat on the journey. At the appointed time the train started rolling and all being well, should be in Duesseldorf at Midnight with just a brief stop at the Dutch/German border. Not long after they had left the quay site at Hook, the light began to fade and it was soon dark. With nothing to see outside Alfred unwrapped cheese rolls, which would be his last meal before getting to Berlin. Then settled down to sleep.

The stop at the border was brief and formal with just some documents changing hands. Alfred soon dropped off to sleep again and it was not until the rhythm of the wheels changed as the train slowed approached Duesseldorf that he awoke from his slumber. As they pulled into the station he saw a lot of people waiting to board the train. "My word," he thought, "we shall be crowded." Alfred need not have worried an equally

236

large number got off the train. After the scheduled 15 minutes wait at 00.15 they were on their way again. "Ah well," said Alfred, "Next stop Berlin!" "Not so," said one of his fellow passengers, "Be prepared for a lengthy stop at the East German border and make sure your papers are all in order." That was one thing Alfred did not have to worry about as he travelled with British authorised papers. Sure enough, when they came to the East German border in the early hours of the morning, it was nearly an hour before they were allowed to proceed on the last part of their journey.

There were no further interruptions for the rest of the journey and the train arrived in Berlin at 05.45 the following morning. The one and only reason Alfred stayed over in Berlin was to see Blondie's family. He knew from Ella's letters that Grete, her mother, was always home in the afternoon. First of all then he was looking for somewhere to have a good breakfast. The last good meal he had eaten was breakfast in the Olympic Village before leaving London. Since then he had made do by having snacks. With Berlin being occupied by four power Allied troops, (American, British, French and Russian) it did not take long for Alfred to find a place to have his first big meal on home ground. He enjoyed his meal and lingered over his second cup of coffee, then used the elaborate toilet facilities to make himself look respectable to make his way to Neu Lichtenberg to meet Blondie's family.

Arriving at the station Alfred asked an official looking man for direction to Rupprecht Strasse. As it happened the man lived locally and was able to direct him. Thankfully it was only a 5 minutes walk and easy to find. Before He entered the building Alfred stopped for a minute wondering what kind of reception he would find. If Ella's mother was alone in the house would she invite a total stranger into their home? There had not been any need to worry, Ella's mother was at home and, after identifying himself, welcomed him with open arms. She made him a cup of coffee and asked Alfred to sit down to stay with her in the kitchen as she wanted to ask lots of questions about Blondie whilst she got on preparing and cooking the meal for the family. The obvious questions, "Is my boy well, is he happy. What is his wife like. Does her family accept him? Alfred assured her that all was well and she need not worry. "Blondie is doing fine."

It was soon after two o'clock when Hilla, the youngest child of the Gruber family got home from school. She was 13 years old and this was her last year at school. Being the age he was, she was a little shy of this stranger in the house, but soon relaxed as she learned more about her brother she could barely remember. She was only three years old when he left home to go to war. It was half an hour later when Otto, the father of the family, came home from work and like the others was equally surprised to see this strange visitor. The meal was ready, and Alfred was invited to stay and share it with the rest of the family. After all, the person he wanted to meet had not returned from work and was unlikely to until later in the evening.

Sure enough, just before six in the afternoon, the lady they all were waiting for got home from work. Unlike the others, Ella guessed at once who the visitor was. After the initial greetings and words of welcome, Mother served Ella with her meal and left the two in the kitchen to talk and get to know each other, whilst she joined papa and Hilla in the sitting room. After Ella had finished eating her meal they too went to sit down, talk some more and ask a lot of questions. Then Ella remembered they needed to find somewhere for Alfred to sleep the night and suggested they pop next door and introduce Alfred to Uncle Paul and Aunty Frieda, who usually put up any unexpected visitors who turned up at the Gruber's. They were pleased to be of help and meet this friend of Blondie's; certainly, this young man could spend the night with them. Back with the family the talking went on until it was time to say good night as everybody had to be up early to go to work, including uncle Paul. Laying in bed and reflecting on the day, which had been a tiring one, Alfred thought what a lovely and warm-hearted family Blondie's relations were. Ella certainly impressed him, a lovely mature woman of 27. These were his last thoughts before he fell asleep.

Six o'clock next morning Uncle Paul came in to wake him, say good bye, wish Alfred well in his search to find his family and start life afresh. After having a wash and getting dressed Alfred said good bye to Aunty Frieda and thanked her for her hospitality before going next door to join the Gruber's for breakfast. Otto had already left and when it was time for Ella to go to the office in the city Alfred took his leave thanking Grete for her kindness in looking after him. Alfred and Ella then made their way to the station to be together for the last few minutes before going their separate ways. Alfred left the train at the Ost Bahnhof promising Ella he would be back for her birthday.

Chapter 32: Sentimental Journey Home

It was not really a sentimental journey home. Home from now on would be where his family found a place to live. The home Alfred left when going to war had been annexed to Poland. Some of the people who lived in those parts stayed behind and became Polish citizens. Those who left gathered as much as they could carry on their journey west across the river Oder seeking a new place to settle, until then they were displaced persons and stateless. Alfred's first objective was to find the platform and track from where the train would depart to take him to Freiberg. He had told Ella in one of his letters that he had lost contact with the family and had no idea where they were.

The Gruber family, having relations in that part of Selisia themselves, heard they had found a home in Freiberg and suggested to Alfred that a good place to start searching for them might be in Freiberg. Here he was on his way to what might turn out to be a fruitless search. The train ran on time and he arrived just after 11 o'clock. After having some lunch Alfred had a stroll through the town centre hoping to find the building housing the municipal offices. Walking past the Rathouse (the town hall), he noticed a sign saying

"Registration of Citizenship 1st floor." Well that's a start should he need to register himself but on going inside the building he saw more direction notices, one reading; "Resident Register" ground floor, room 12. Now that was what he was really looking for, what luck. The staff were very pleasant and helpful. Alfred told them that he was looking for his family and he name was Zollman. After a moment looking for the register containing citizens whose name began with B, it took only moments to find the name Zollman. Yes, there were two entries by that name. After Alfred supplied more detailed information he was shown an entry for a displaced family by that name registered and living in Freiberg since 1946 at 36 Branderstrasse. The person dealing with Alfred suggested he might have alook at the town's plan displayed in the entrance hall. It was very detailed and Branderstrasse was not far away and 15 minutes later he was standing outside a block of flats wondering what he would find.

Alfred knocked firmly at the front door of flat 6 and it was only moments later that the door opened and his mother could hardly believe what she saw. Her first born back from the war! Needless to say both were overjoyed and emotional, with their tears flowing freely. Once Alfred was inside Alma wanted to know all about his time in England, Alfred's general well being and many more things.

All Alfred wanted was to sit down' have a cup of coffee and a bite to eat. Alma soon supplied her son's needs, had a cup of coffee herself and then sitting next to her son asked endless questions. Alfred answered them by just saying yes or no at the time but leaving the fuller answers until they were all together having their evening meal.

Whilst mother was preparing and cooking the evening meal Alfred picked up his luggage and went up to his brother Karl's bedroom which they now had to share, and put his few belongings away. Some furniture had to be moved to a new position to create space for the extra bed, which was to be a camp bed stored at the back of the cupboard. Once every thing was in its place Alfred went down to the kitchen and joined his mother and Karl as well as his father and other brother, Rudy, who had arrived home from work. All were overjoyed to see Alfred and happy to have him home again. Over the meal Alfred answered all their questions in as much detail as they needed to know. He also told them about his stop-over in Berlin. To call on his friend Blondie's family. After the meal they all sat around the room discussing the future and Werner pointed out to Alfred the first thing he needed to do was to get new identity papers and register his residency in Freiberg. Without them he would be unable to draw any financial social assistance. Neither could he enrol on any retraining courses to find work in any of the professions or trades which the regular soldier returning from the war needed. Alfred thanked his father for his good advice. Alma looked at her oldest son and noticed he had a job to keep awake and suggested he had better go to bed so as to be fresh and rested in the morning for all the interviews he would face the following day. She would go with him as she knew she would be of some help to Alfred. After all it was not so many months ago that the rest of the family had to go through the same procedure. Not only was the family homeless at the time but also stateless as the Polish authorities had confiscated all their identity papers.

Next morning came all too soon for Alfred but he knew the sooner he got into the queue the sooner the job would get done. First stop however was at the photographer, he knew from experience all these documents he was applying for required photos of the applicant. With little money in his pocket his mother kindly footed the bill as she did for the registration. Proving his identity was easier than he had expected as the clerk dealing with his application accepted the discharge paper issued by the British authorities as sufficient proof of identity. Next stop Social Services; same building different floor. Here the queue was a little longer but it did not take too long before a lady attended to his needs. With all the boxes ticked Alfred was granted the standard allowance for a single person. All done, the lady handed him a payslip for the amount he could draw from the cashier on the way out. She also gave Alfred a list of firms that had vacancies to be filled as well as a list giving the firms that were running training courses paid for by the Borough of Freiberg.

Well, Alfred thought that was quick and painless. He gave his mother an affectionate kiss, took her by the arm and went along the road to the nearest Café to treat her to a cup of coffee and a cake. Whilst Alma was enjoying her coffee and cake Alfred had a quick glance over the list offering retraining courses and found very quickly what he was looking for; Electro plumber in the manufacturing of refrigerators sounded good to him. Spending a considerable time with the Americans in Italy, it was quite clear, now the war was over it would be the refrigerator that was the household item every family must have. That was the training he was after and he told his mother so and suggested she go home now and he would pop across town to the company manufacturing refrigerators and see if he could enrol in the next training course.

Alfred admitted to himself that he felt more than just a little tense, since he had no manufacturing experience. What was the company looking for anyway? Again, luck had not forsaken him. The two men interviewing him were very understanding knowing full well that young men of Alfred's generation knew nothing but war and had not had the time to learn a profession or trade. What they were most impressed with was his war record and with that alone they would have enrolled him. After a few more questions they told him to go to the general office and enrol for the two-week course commencing the following Monday.

In the evening when the family was together again talking through the day's events, all were pleased to hear Alfred's news about training for a new occupation, adding new skills to the ones the Army had taught him. Already he had a good knowledge of the working and maintenance of two and four stroke petrol engines as well as the driving skills. Alfred saw that in future nobody could live without a car and a fridge in the house. Yes, on reflection the future looked bright and the family agreed with him. Knowing now that the course would end on 25th June he could keep his date with Ella on her 27th birthday and he wrote and told her so.

The remaining few days of the week passed very quickly and the following Monday Alfred reported at the factory with great confidence, eager to learn more about refrigeration. Equally the lecturers, engineers and foremen alike were eager to see how the new class would grasp the skills they were being taught. There was no doubt that way out in front was Alfred.

At the end of the course, the pass certificate issued to Alfred also included a report stating his amazing mental strength of comprehending and retaining what was being taught and to expand on it. The outcome of it all was that the management offered Alfred a permanent job with the firm starting 1st July 1948. Secretly that was what Alfred has hoped for as he intended to ask Ella to marry him when next he saw her on her birthday.

Chapter 33: Married Bliss

In the days before his trip to Berlin, Alfred had looked into the window of some Jewellery shops in town to select an engagement ring for Ella. They all looked totally different from what he could remember before the war, not that he was interested in them before he joined the Para Troopers. Eventually he saw one he liked hoping that Ella would like it as well but he would soon find out for sure in a few days time, Alfred had arranged with Ella that he would be in Berlin on 27th June and return home on the 29th to get himself ready for his new job starting on the 1st July.

With time to spare after arriving in Berlin and before making his way to Lichtenberg, Alfred decided to give Ella a surprise by going to her office, waiting till she finished work and then they would go home together. There was a small park area opposite the office building where he could wait and watch the world go by. It was, after all, midsummer and sitting for half an hour or so would not do him any harm. The afternoon had turned out to be very warm and sultry and it seemed not very long before the ladies came out of the building making their way home. Imagine the joy in both their hearts when Alfred's plan of surprise worked. Ella's colleagues wanted to know who this young, handsome man was. So she introduced him as Alfred, a friend she had met through her brother and whom she had invited to her birthday. She knew then there would be a lot of leg pulling in the next few days at the office. When the two young lovers got home, Ella's mother was pleased to see them both as she had expected Alfred earlier in the afternoon. With papa being on late shift the family were all present so they could have their evening meal straight away.

The rest of the evening was very relaxing specially for Alfred as he felt quite at home with the ladies, each airing their views about the future as they would like it to be. All too soon Grete reminded them that tomorrow would be a long and tiring day as these birthdays were in the Gruber family. When Alfred woke the next morning he could not believe his eyes,08.15! Why had not someone called him? Aunt Frieda told him he was sound asleep and neither Uncle Paul nor herself had the heart to wake him. Once up and dressed Alfred had breakfast with Aunt Frieda and spent the rest of the morning with her learning much about Ella's family background. Just before lunch he popped in to see Grete and say hello before taking the train to Alexandra Platz where the clearing of rubble went on apace so further reconstruction work could begin. He had a look at the two newly opened department stores before making his way to Ella's offices to wish her a happy birthday which he had failed to do in the morning. He did not have to wait long before the ladies emerged and he went to Ella gave her a hearty kiss and wished her a happy birthday to applause from all who stood around.

When they arrived home a number of the family had already arrived. "My", Alfred thought, "this is going to be a lively party," as he had no idea of the number of cousins there were. He had a sneaky idea though that the large turn out was partly to meet him as well as celebrating Ella's birthday. Before long Grete invited them to get their food from the kitchen and enjoy themselves, all this was standard family routine but to Alfred an entirely new experience.

Meal over, a toast to the birthday child before the generations divided with the older members of the family going into the little room and the younger ones taking over the slightly larger one. First job as ever was rolling back the carpet before dancing could begin. Usually Blondie and Ella would start the dancing, but Blondie being absent, the older brother Reinhold did the honours. After that it was free for all. Throughout the evening Alfred wondered when the right moment was to propose marriage to Ella, and it eventually came when mama brought in the birthday cake. Whilst everybody was munching away and there was a moment of quiet, Alfred seized his opportunity, took the ring out of his pocket, turned to Ella and without any ceremony asked her if she would marry him. There was only a moment of hesitation before she gave a positive "Yes"; which gave cause for another toast to be drunk. Everybody in the family wished them well. At 22.00 the party broke up and people made their way home, after all tomorrow was another working day.

Alfred and Ella were quite relieved after everybody had left. They were also quite excited about the prospect of being together for the rest of their lives and tiredness and sleep were far away. As it was a warm, dry and sultry night they decide to take a walk in the nearby park to have a moment to themselves before going to bed. Perhaps in retrospect they wished they hadn't.

Chapter 34: Happy Family Life

The following morning Alfred made sure he was up in time to say good bye to Ella before she went work. He would be on the train home to Freiberg about mid-day and when he got home his mother wanted to know how it had all gone. "Fine thank you, it all went very well". That was all his mother could get out of him. It was when all the Zollman family had their evening meal together that he told them that he had proposed marriage to Ella and she had accepted his proposal. "Any idea when you are getting married?" Werner ventured to ask. "Sometime next spring," Alfred replied. What the two young lovers thought was that they would meet once a month either in Berlin or Freiberg and at some time soon the two sets of parents would arrange to meet. Freiberg might be the better choice, Otto working for the railways could travel free and so could Grete.

The wedding day was the last thing on Alfred's mind at the moment. First he wanted to do his best at the factory hoping it would lead to a permanent contract and with it a little higher pay packet. Secondly before long he would start looking for a small flat somewhere in town where he and Ella would be alone, away from glaring eyes of the family. As far as work was concerned Alfred found no difficulty or stress doing the job and after only after a day or two was quite relaxed and happy, getting on with his workmates extremely well, but then that was his nature. The Army had known what he was capable of and for a good reason posted him to help with the training of new recruits. He was also a good leader hence when being prisoner in Italy he had attained the rank of Staff Sergeant. All this did not go unnoticed by his bosses who were very pleased to have him on their staff.

Under such happy circumstances the weeks flew by and soon it was time to pack his little overnight bag and spend another week-end in Berlin. He really was longing to see Ella again, so he took the overnight train for them to have the maximum time together. Alfred began to know his way around Berlin now and had no difficulty in taking the right train from the right platform. He got to the Gruber's home just after 09.00 and enjoyed the breakfast Grete offered him. An hour later the two of them found themselves in town, window shopping, looking for items needed to set up a home of their own. During their lunch break from shopping Ella leaned across the table, took Alfred's hand in hers, looked into his eyes and said; "Darling I am pregnant!" Alfred was lost for words for a moment as the words Ella whispered to him raced through his mind. In a way he could not be more pleased with this news. He was 27 years and old enough to be a father and raise a family, on the other hand he was furious with himself that his dream to set up home before having children had gone awry. Well what is done is done. Future plans had to be changed. The first priority was to arrange a wedding day. It was now August and the earliest they could get married was October as it took 8 weeks for all the legal documents to be in place. When asking Ella how she felt about it all, she too was happy bearing a child, at her age it was time she did. When breaking the news to Ella's parents, mama could not have been more pleased. To papa, a wedding in October would mean he would loose his daughter earlier than expected. Before leaving for home the next day, arrangements were made for Ella and her parents to go to Freiberg and meet Alfred's family.

On the way back to Freiberg Alfred wondered how his parents would receive the news of becoming grandparents. He knew his mother would be pleased but not quite so sure how his father would take it. So it turned out, Alma was pleased there was a grandchild on the way but Werner let it be known it would have been better if Alfred had shown more self control, as nothing could be done about it he would do his best to help them. Alfred was very thankful that his parents took the news the way they did, and it was now up to him to help Ella settle in her new role when she came to Freiberg.

The meeting between the two sets of parents when the Gruber's came to Freiberg, went extremely well. The two fathers put the world to rights whilst between the mums there was just baby talk. In fact they all got on well together. Before Otto and Grete returned to Berlin they told Alfred's parents they would look after all the wedding arrangements, so they were not to worry. In fact they were looking forward to welcoming them to Berlin in October which was not all that far away. Alfred managed to see his bride only once more before the wedding. Ella looked radiant. She had got over her morning sickness and indeed was looking forward to being a mother.

Chapter 35: Parenthood

As the wedding day dawned Alfred was quite tense and understandably so. It was not every day a man gets married and after all it is a big step to take in any one's life, man or woman. As the time of the ceremony drew nearer Alfred relaxed and when he saw Ella outside the magistrate's offices he knew he had made the right decision. Fortunately the ceremony was brief and only the parents were present with the two fathers acting as witnesses.

Whist the bride and groom and their parents were with the marriage registrar the rest of the family put the final touches to the marriage feast. When the newlyweds arrived, the musicians welcomed them with traditional songs and music and got the feast on the way. Only members of Ella's family living in the eastern sector of Berlin were at the wedding as the younger people   living in the western sectors were reluctant to cross the border as no one could guarantee their safety not knowing what the East German authorities would be up to next. Nonetheless it was a happy occasion and the party went on until ten o'clock in the evening when people started leaving for home although Ella and Alfred left earlier to stay at a hotel nearby to get some rest. Also, they needed to be up and about early next day to catch the train back to Freiberg.

Back in their little flat it take not long for life to establish a routine. Alfred left home for work just after six each morning to be at the factory in good time to clock in. Work finished at 17.00 and he was usually back home just after 17.30. Ella was lucky to find a part-time job as a secretary for four hours a day, five days a week from 09.00- 13.00. That gave her time to have a little rest before cooking the evening meal. Supper over, Alfred always helped with clearing the table and the washing up before putting his feet up for what he considered his well deserved rest. There was just one exception, Friday evenings when he went to his local for a beer, but mostly to play his favourite card game Skat. Saturday mornings they went out shopping and in the afternoon went to see Alma, Alfred's mother, who kept an eye on Ella carrying the first grand child of the Zollman's family. Alfred and Ella were truly excited of becoming parents. Neither could imagine not having children around them.

Everybody was happy the way things had settled down. Life ahead seemed like a bed of roses. Christmas came and went and everybody was wondering how 1949 would turn out. One thing Alfred knew was, that he would become a father and was looking forward to this experience. Ella had given up work and would concentrate and prepare the best she could for motherhood. The baby was due at the end of March or early April. As the time drew near Alfred became quite tense hoping all would go well. He had given up going to his local on Friday evenings as somehow he was unable to concentrate on playing cards. Even at work he dare not think of anything other than his job in hand.

When the time came Ella delivered a healthy baby boy. She herself, apart from being tired, felt very well. Even the staff attending to her remarked how well she had coped with her first delivery. Alma too was thankful all had gone well but secretly had hoped it would be a grand-daughter as she herself was the mother of three sons. Bringing up the baby however would be a new experience for Alfred and he had to learn a great deal on this subject. As his past had shown Alfred learns quickly and bringing up baby was no exception.

Before long life dropped back into its old routine. The baby was healthy and all the Zollman family spoiled the new arrival. At the factory too Alfred's bosses were impressed with his dedication to any job they asked him to do which resulted in a small wage rise and a promotion of sorts, as the management put him on a bench where they inspected fridges which had to be taken off the production line because of some fault or other. Around the time of Ella's birthday she conceived again. That pleased both of them because Ella had all along said she wanted more than just the one child and here it was on the way. Parents too received the news with joy. Everybody was happy, so what else could you ask of life.

The same could not be said about the political scene. Russian influence on the course the new German Socialist Republic should take became more evident by the week. More and more East Germans attempted to escape to the West for a better, freer life. The outcome, guards along the border with West Germany were increased and so were the checking points. Documents underwent greater scrutiny and anyone under sixty years old stood little chance of crossing unless they had a compelling reason, such as official business with the West. Many accepted the situation, hundreds did not. In their determination to escape they made their way to a lonely place along the border and under cover of darkness tried to slip across into West Germany knowing there was always the danger of being detected by a passing patrol. From the hundreds who attempted to cross the line, relatively few were successful. Those who used the Russian Sector in East

Berlin to escape from East German regime did not fare much better. It was only a short border and well lit on both sides. Those who were brave enough to take this route by attempting to swim across the river Spree to freedom in the West, were practically committing suicide. Records showed that of many of those who took to the water, only a few made it alive. Alfred felt for those men and women as many endured much hardship during the war. There was little he could do to help these people. For the time being he was content, happily married, a family to raise with another baby on the way, he had better make the most of what he had.

Another Christmas went by. Another New Year rung in. At work the company widened its production manufacturing as many fridges for the commercial and military market as it did for the domestic market. That meant an additional production line. Alfred was transferred to this new work with the purpose of helping the new and additional labour force needed to get this new line into full production as quickly as possible. With it came a small pay rise which was most welcome in the Zollman's household. For the average household to purchase a fridge, most needed to save up for it and that could take several weeks; this new market was welcomed by management and workers alike. As 1950 progressed there was only one topic;

Baby Talk. Will the new baby be a girl this time or will it be another boy? Grandmother Alma hoped it would be a girl. Ella and Alfred hoped it would be a healthy, bouncing baby whatever the gender and that mother would be well after the delivery. That was what the family in Berlin also hoped for. Then early in May Ella delivered her second baby, another boy. Ella found grandmother Alma a great help in looking after two infants. Alfred too took his fatherhood seriously and as before gave up his Friday evenings playing cards with his friends at the local.

On the political scene, as far as the government of the German Democratic Republic was concerned, if they wanted to hold on to their position of power they had better do as Moscow told them. That meant they were nothing but puppets in Russian hands. Alfred did not like it one little bit. Europe had just been freed from the claws of one dictator only to be replaced by another oppressive regime. As under Hitler, you dared not air your views or speak out against the government, or say anything that might be misinterpreted. The danger for Alfred, after a few drinks on Friday evenings, now that he had returned to his old routine, was the temptation to speak more freely. Telling the people at the bar how wonderful it is to live in a democratic country where you could speak freely on any matter including politics. His father and friends warned him to be more careful about what he was saying and suggested he count up to ten before he said anything. There may come a day, they warned him, he might regret not having guarded his tongue. He had to remember he had a wife and children who relied on him. All sounded good advice but when you are passionate for living under democratic rules, a way of life millions died for, how can you keep quiet? Then one day it happened, Alfred spoke rather accusingly about the government's new rules and laws, mainly on supporting the Russian forces stationed in East Germany. What was left for the German people was nothing less than the crumbs under the table.

Not surprisingly Alfred's remarks did not go down too well with the hardened socialists at the bar, all members of the Communist party. A strong verbal argument started between Alfred and the party members coming to the point where physical punches were exchanged. That was when Alfred's father and two friends intervened to drag Alfred away and tell him to beat it and go into hiding as the police were sure to look for him now. Alfred did not go into hiding but went straight home. He had previously discussed such a situation with Ella. Should it ever come to pass he would go to Berlin and hopefully make it across the border into West Berlin.

When he got home and told Ella what had happened, she was shocked but not surprised as she knew her husband's strong views on this matter only too well. Alfred gathered some changes of clothing and the warmest coat he had, as he might have to spend a night or two out in the open. Ella handed him the rail fare to Berlin, they kissed passionately good bye and he then left her and the boys to fate. Alfred's hope was that he would be on his way before the police started looking for him nationwide. Once he was on the train he would be pretty safe until he arrived in Berlin. There were a few scary moments for Alfred. Every time the train came to a halt his heart began to beat faster wondering whether the news of his arrest had caught up with him, but no, as far as he could see only passengers left or boarded the train.

It was Saturday morning when he got off the train at the Ost Bahnhof. Alfred, from previous visits, knew the station, and indeed the whole area very well by now. With Lady Luck on his side he could avoid being spotted by the police, and Lady Luck was on his side. Once away from the station he made straight for Lichtenberg, the family home and told them of his plight. It was but a brief visit and they arranged to meet after dark at the park nearby at the far end where the young people did their courting. With that he was gone. Otto and Grete discussed the situation and decided to send Hilla to Reinhold and let him know what had happened. Reinhold apart from Hilla was the only other child of the Gruber family that lived in Berlin. Both brother and sister knew Berlin like the back of their hand and if anyone could get to the border undetected it was these two. After a brief discussion all four agreed that if their plan to get Alfred to, and across the line, was to succeed it had to be sooner rather than later - this very night in fact. The fewer people who knew about this plan all this the better. Hilla, for the love of her sister, was prepared to do what ever the family thought was the best way out of this unexpected and unwelcome situation.

When the time came Reinhold and Hilla went to the park and met Alfred and told him what the plan was. If he was not happy with what was proposed then going into hiding for a long period was the only alternative. Alfred did not hesitate, He was a risk taker and adventurer and immediately said: "Let's Go. Let's do it!" "For all our sakes I hope you do it," answered Reinhold. Then he left leaving Hilla to explain to Alfred what was proposed. A quarter of an hour later the two went on their way. It was all on foot, some 6 miles or so, through dimly lit back streets over rubble and through bombed out buildings. The point chosen where Alfred might cross into West Berlin was the northern end bordering the French sector. Very little reconstruction had been done in his part and there was no street lighting. For Alfred's plan it could not be better. The border was only a few yards away now and Hilla suggested to wait and make sure the right moment would be chosen to make the leap into freedom. Failure could mean death or long imprisonment. Waiting a while paid off. An open car with four occupants, two Russians soldiers and two East German police went by checking the fence for any gaps. When the rear lights of the car had disappeared Hilla alerted Alfred and said: "Go for it!" With that Alfred sprinted the short distance to the border taking the fence by storm as he had done a number of times in the battles of Monte Casino. Apart from a tear or two in his clothing he was O.K. landing on the other side. He needed to move away from the dividing line as fast as his feet could carry him in case he was spotted by some other watchman who might have a shot at him. Fortunately this area in the French sector was not very brightly lit and within two minutes he was out of rifle range and safe. Alfred stopped for a minute to get his breath, then looked back to where he had just come from and could still see the fence, the demarcation line between east and west. Further along the line towards the Brandenburg Gate, he could see the bright lights illuminating the sky. Yes he made it thanks to Ella's family especially Hilla, his sister in law.

Chapter 36: The Final Road to Freedom

To travel the road to freedom proved not to be an easy one. It was uneven and full of potholes, had its ups and downs and sometimes even mountains to climb. It also brought stress and hardship to the families back in East Germany. Alfred had expected to encounter some problems but not to the scale he was confronted with now. He knew the first thing to do was to report to the police and claim political asylum. By taking this step he became a stateless person. He deliberately left home without identification papers to delay being taken into custody should he be arrested on the way by the East German police. It was sometime before he saw a police patrol who listened carefully to his story and then took him to the nearest police station. There they handed Alfred over to the officer on duty who asked him a few more questions before locking him into a cell and indicating that his future would be dealt with in the morning. The duty officer then asked one of his colleagues to get the prisoner in cell 4 some coffee and a bite to eat.

After spending the night in a police cell and eating a good breakfast, Alfred was taken before a Magistrate and the proof of identity procedure began. He had been through a similar experience not all that long ago and had a good idea what questions might be asked so he was ready and explained in detail how it came about that he now found himself in this situation. The Magistrate listened sympathetically and explained to Alfred that this time he was in court as a political asylum seeker and not registering as a demobilized soldier returning from the war. To grant someone citizenship was a serious matter and proof of character was needed. "Who would speak for you and testify that you are Alfred Zollman as you claim to be." "Well," Alfred answered: "There is my war record." Alfred gave the court the details and the Magistrate accepted that these records might help and adjourned the sitting for two days.

Two days later the court sat again with the Magistrate having scrutinised Alfred's war record, and opened procedures by saying: "Most impressive." Then he questioned Alfred in detail about time and places in his war record. By the end of the question and answer session the Magistrate was satisfied that the man before him was Alfred Zollman and his application for citizenship was genuine and recommended his application to go before a Notary for it to become legal. A meeting with a Notary was arranged and a week later Alfred officially became a

West German citizen. He was also offered a bed-sitter for a month, rent free, to allow him time to find a job and new accommodation as well as a generous amount of one off spending money to get started. This was indeed a moment to celebrate, but with his wife and children the other side of the fence and not knowing what measure the authorities had taken in retaliation, there was not much left to celebrate.

In his loneliness Alfred made his way back to his bed-sitter and had a long think about what to do next. Getting in touch with the family in Lichtenberg was not advisable. He remembered there was a brother of Grete living in West Berlin and a first cousin of Ella's. But where, he could not remember. Alfred recalled however that the brother worked for the Berlin City Council as a dustbin collector. If he went to the depot early in the morning he might get the chance to have a quick word with him and so he did. He met Ella's uncle and he told him that the family in the west had heard about his problem and escape but the news from the east was not good. Alfred was told both families, in Freiberg and Berlin, had paid the price for his escape to the west. The East German Authority was ruthless in its retaliation, making an example of them and warning the people what would happen to them if they tried the same thing

When Alfred returned to his quarters and re-assessed the situation it became obvious that there was not anything he could do to help his wife and children. From what he gathered both families were watched as soon as they left the house. Reinhold in fact came under 24 hour surveillance because of his knowledge of the latest developments in communication skills and how to use them to the best advantage and also how to install the electronic modern equipment in government buildings and establishments. Here was someone the government did not want to lose. Being watched day and night became very stressful for Reinhold and his family with his mother watching her son with dismay as he was on the brink of a total nervous breakdown.

In Freiberg the situation had become unbearable for Ella. Alma and Werner had sacrificed enough. She was almost at breaking point. But because of her two boys dare not give in. She saw only one way out, Berlin. Ella had heard about their plight of being watched, and her appearance at the family home might make matters worse, yet she could see no other way out of her situation. The family had been through this before, during the war. Their motto; united we stand. As soon as she had enough money for the train fare she left Freiberg with the children hoping for good fortune for her journey back home to Berlin. When Otto opened the door he could hardly recognise his daughter. The woman before him was thin, gaunt looking with no colour in her cheeks. It was from her voice when falling around his neck to kiss him that he eventually recognised her. When Grete arrived back from her shopping she was equally surprised to see Ella and the state she was in. Her instinct told her the three needed careful nursing before any plans could be made for their future

Alfred was told by the family in the west of Ella and the boys being in Lichtenberg. Hearing about this he was tempted to risk a crossing back to the east to see his family but was strongly advised against it. When the time was right they would find the ways and means of getting there. Just be patient he was told. That was one thing lacking in Alfred's character. From now on priority was finding the right job. Good, permanent work was hard to find as he did not have the necessary skills to fill any vacancies. It was very depressing for Alfred when he looked around and all the family here in Berlin had good, well paid jobs, for him it was casual labour or work on building sites or on sick pay. The worry about the future, not eating enough nor eating the right food, resulted in spells of sickness. Which all amounted to a smaller weekly income. That worried Alfred a great deal. Would he ever have enough income to keep the family? Then in the spring of 1951, just before Easter, one of Ella's first cousins came to see him at his new address on the western outskirts of the city, an apartment large enough for the family to live in, to tell him of the plan to get his wife and boys into West Berlin at a time when the check points are very busy. It would be on Easter Day a day when citizens from both sides of the divide wanted to see family members on the other side of the line. To avoid long queues and any unrest in the crowd the past had shown, that officials would only glance at the identity papers and wave them through. After all it was Easter, the great Christian Festival. Alfred himself had to stay away, in fact stay home. Ella and the children as soon as they crossed the line would get into the nearest parked car, one of three standing by, and come straight to this address. Just pray all goes well. This was on Palm Sunday, so he had a week to get organised. Maundy Thursday was the last working day and also pay day. That would not give him much time for shopping, it would be best to ask little aunt Emma if she could help him to give Ella the welcome and meal she deserved.

On Easter day one could feel the tension in the Gruber household as Ella got ready to leave home, maybe for the last time and hoping the plan of

272

attempting to get her and the children to the west would succeed. This was make or break day. Could she keep calm at the checkpoint and not give the game away. She also had to travel light with little or no luggage as this may give rise to suspicion. Yet she needed some luggage for the boys at least. Just pray she told herself, there would be crowds of people about and if needed she could act convincingly. To leave the family out of it a trusted friend took her as close as she could to the check point. It was 11.00 when they got out of the car There was quite a crowd waiting to get across to see their dear ones, and growing by the minute. So far so good and may it continue. People around Ella were very kind some let her go ahead of them in front of the queue, because of the children, and spoke to the boys. People behind her were crowding impatiently in on the check point and true enough, the official just looked at the photo in the passport, then looked at Ella, stamped the document, and let them through. What concerned Ella at that moment was, could she keep her nerve. Having to keep an eye on the boys helped. Cousin Egbert too prayed he would keep his nerves as he casually came and walked beside Ella, putting his arm around her and said: "Keep walking." It had fallen on Egbert to take the cousins to their new home which Alfred had prepared for them as he happened to be parked nearest the check point crossing. It was 11.47 when they got into the car and set out to the family's new home.

The reunion when she met Alfred was a joyous and emotional one and both had tears in their eyes. Aunt Emma and cousin Egbert realised there was no point staying on. After saying good bye they made their way home and left the family to themselves. It took a little while for the couple to calm down before they had their special Sunday lunch. The boys too needed feeding and attention. Alfred apologised to Ella for his thoughtless action which had caused her so much suffering. He could see she was not the blooming young woman he had left in Freiberg. The boys on the other hand had grown and developed enormously since he had seen them last. Ella soon settled down in her new surroundings and it did not take her long to change the apartment into a home. Being happy and content she was soon her old self again both in spirit and in looks.

Alfred carried on with his various jobs, working on building sites, some part-time work and casual labour, earning as much money as he could. Later that year Ella became pregnant again and Alfred was desperate to find a better paid job. As luck would have it he heard from an old veteran that the American supply depot were looking for suitable men to be employed as guards. Now there was a job that would suit him. Without delay he obtained an application form, filled it in and returned it to the American Headquarters in the city. It took a a long time before he had a reply but when he did receive it it contained good news. It requested him to appear for an interview at the headquarters, Roosevelt Barracks, Berlin Command. At the appointed time Alfred presented himself before the selection panel who asked him very pertinent questions about his war service and his time as a P.oW. All of which Alfred was happy to answer. He had the impression the panel was very intrigued with his 2 tours on the Russian front. After a few more general questions about his family and other interests they ended the interview with the familiar words, "You will hear from us in a few days." That was all Alfred expected to hear. Fortunately he did not have to wait for too long as three days later, returning from work, Ella handed him an envelope from USA Headquarters Berlin, which informed him he had been accepted for employment as a guard and he was to report for training commencing on the first of April. This news did lift a weight not only off Alfred's shoulder but Ella's as well; a regular and permanent job with a little extra weekly income as well. Here was something Alfred was really good at. In his 6 years as a soldier he did many hours of guard duty.

When he arrived at the depot and entered the lecture room he was surprised at the number of men who were to be recruited but the reason soon became clear as the day went on. The supply depot covered three quarters of the site of a very large US Army camp. The last quarter was the garrison, run quite independently of the supply depot which was to be guarded 24 hours a day. This would mean shift work with a 5-day working week and 2 rest days and there would be four groups working in rotation. Work would commence on the 15th April with the first shift starting at 06.00. This would mean the first train or tram would get him to work on time. The late shift could still get home before trams and trains stopped for the night. Duty rotas would be handed to them when they were leaving. Well, Alfred thought that is something the family has to get used to, as he had already set his heart on this job. The night shift had little to do apart from doing the rounds to see that all was well. When on duty during the day checking validity of drivers' documents kept him busy.

When the newness of the job had worn off Alfred found the job rather boring as he was used to more life and activity around him and said so to Ella who was not surprised as she knew her man. One evening when reading the papers he came across an Australian government advert for assisted passage to a new life in Australia. Turning to Ella he remarked; "Ever thought of emigrating?" "Not really," she answered "What brought that on?" "Come and see," was Alfred's reply. Both then looked at the advert more closely and what the Australian government, apart from the assistant passage, offered the applicant and immigrant on arrival. On the top of the list was the guarantee of a job for the minimum of at least 2 years with the pay being almost double that which could be earned in Berlin by doing equivalent work. Free accommodation for 6 months but this could be extended. All Australian laws and rights would apply from the day they landed. "Sounds too good to be true." said Ella. "O, I don't know. Let's sleep on it and talk some more before making any firm decision" were Alfred's final words on the matter.

The idea of a new life in Australia went round and round in Alfred's mind. His spirit of adventure was stirred up and he could do little to calm it. Eventually the couple sat down and put on paper the advantages and disadvantages of remaining in Berlin and immigrating. What had Australia to offer? A lot more than Berlin was the answer. The decision was made and papers from the Australian embassy in Bonn applied for. Having filled in the forms and returned them to the Australian embassy in Bonn they did not have to wait long for a reply. Subject to a health check, they were accepted. The health check raised no concern since the whole family was fit, even the baby, yet another boy, born in 1952 was thriving in the Berlin air.

The night before they left Berlin there was a farewell party but sadly, some of the younger family members living in East Berlin, Hilla and Reinhold and others were missing. So it was rather a low key affair. Otto was sad to see his daughter go and Grete to lose some of the family. Perhaps it was just as well for the Zollman family. They had to make an early start the following morning to catch the plane which took them to the port of embarkation. After arrival at the port they were taken to a large shed on the quay where identity papers were checked and boarding cards issued, then straight on to the ship. Most of the crew were at hand and seeing them to their cabins. The Zollman's had two cabins adjoining each other with a connecting door. Departure time was 16.00 and on the dot the ship slipped away from the quay. On the open decks passengers waved goodbye to the people left behind. There were tears in everyones eyes including Alfred's. This was what the 6 years of fighting during the war had achieved. - To escape poverty and live in a country where you were free, a country full of opportunities and where you had a say in how people should be governed. It was this way of life that millions had fought and died for in the effort.

Epilogue

There may be a number of questions people will be asking after having read this book. Firstly; why have we not heard or read about these young soldiers before? The answer, they never talked about it. To them it was all done in the line of duty. It was not until after they died that their relatives came across diaries and other writings revealing their war records showing the ranks they had attained and medals and other honours presented to them.

Some may wish to know how Vincent came into the picture when the book is about Alfred. The answer to that is, the author knew both men and learned that these two young men had almost identical war records. Both were born in 1921, both volunteered to join the armed forces in their respective countries in 1939 when 18 years of age. Vincent, his family believes, even had a German pen-friend before the war. Both served in elite units throughout the war. Both saw active service, Alfred had two tours in Russia, Vincent two tours in North Africa. Both were dispatch riders and both fought in Greece, Crete and the Italian campaign, most likely facing one another as they certainly did on Crete. Possibly facing each other somewhere in Italy. Both were taken P o W twice. Alfred was freed by German troops on the first occasion and escaped after being taken prisoner by the Americans the second time. Vincent on the other hand, being ordered to surrender to the Germans escaped a few days later. Back in North Africa, after being captured by the Italians forces outside Tobruk he made no attempt to break out. On returning to England he was interviewed by MI5 who wanted to know why he did not escape on that occasion, to which Vincent replied, he did not see any sense in escaping that time as he knew the strength of the Allied forces and the reluctance of the Italians to fight he could see Allied victory in less than two weeks, and so it proved to be.

Both men received campaign medals as recognition for their services to the cause and their bravery. Vincent's medals; 1939 - 1945 war Medal, 1939 - 1945 star, The African Star, the Italian Star, The France and Germany star. In 2016 at the age of 95 he was awarded the Legion d'honneur by the French government. On D-Day, with thousands of other troops, Vincent landed on the Normandy beaches, again deployed as a dispatch rider. His services here were rather short as soon after D-day, when delivering urgent messages he hit a landmine and damaged his legs beyond repair. Both legs had to be amputated making further participation in the war impossible.

Alfred too received recognition for his services, the most treasured, the armband indicating he was engaged in the bloody battle of Crete. Only members of the Parachute Regiment actually fighting on the island were awarded this honour. He was also awarded the Iron Cross 2nd class twice as well as the Iron Cross1^{st} Class. Alfred was presented with medals for each time he was wounded, the rank when he was discharged from the German armed forces, Staff Sergeant. Having read the book you will know Alfred could not settle in post-war Germany and with his family emigrated to Australia where he found what he was looking for; freedom, happiness and peace. His earthly remains are interred in a garden of peace owned and run by a Buddhist community in Australia.

Vincent's `rehabilitation took 19 months at the end of which he was fitted with prosthetics and trained as a cobbler, but found there was not enough work to earn a living. Looking for work he came across a veteran from W.W.1 who told him that the Post Office were looking for telephone operators. He applied and got the job. He retired as a supervisor from the telephone service in 1981. He met his future wife who was lodging with his mother in Basingstoke. She took him out for walks in the park in his wheelchair. Love blossomed and they got married. They married at St. Mary's Fratton Park, Portsmouth. Vincent walked down the long aisle, and it is a long walk, in his newly fitted legs. They had two children, a boy and girl. The garden was Vincent's hobby and his pride and joy. He died aged 96 and is buried at Holly Hill cemetery at Sarisbury Green in Hampshire next to his wife. These are just two accounts and there are thousands more where men acted on the spur of the moment and saved the day. Their heroic actions saved not only the day and lives but who knows may have even won the battle and ultimately won the war. Your grandfather may have been one of them.